The Literacy Leadership Guide for Elementary Principals

The Literacy Leadership Guide for Elementary Principals

Reclaiming Teacher Autonomy and Joy

Tynisha D. Meidl
Jason Lau
Margaret-Mary Sulentic Dowell

ROWMAN & LITTLEFIELD
Lanham • Boulder • New York • London

Published by Rowman & Littlefield
An imprint of The Rowman & Littlefield Publishing Group, Inc.
4501 Forbes Boulevard, Suite 200, Lanham, Maryland 20706
www.rowman.com

Unit A, Whitacre Mews, 26-34 Stannary Street, London SE11 4AB

British Library Cataloguing in Publication Information Available

Library of Congress Cataloging-in-Publication Data Available

ISBN 9781475840902 (electronic) | ISBN 9781475840889 (cloth : alk. paper) | ISBN
    9781475840896 (pbk. : alk. paper)

♾ ™ The paper used in this publication meets the minimum requirements of American National Standard for Information Sciences Permanence of Paper for Printed Library Materials, ANSI/NISO Z39.48-1992.

Printed in the United States of America

Contents

Foreword

Dana L. Bickmore

The interaction of teacher and student, often termed the *core technology* of schooling, is a highly complex, iterative process. This interactive process is particularly complex as students learn to become literate. Literacy skills are foundational, in any culture, as students move through school systems and engage in society as adults. There is no lack of research or understanding by the public of the importance of literacy learning.

The importance of the principal, however, is far less researched or understood in relationship to supporting the *core technology* of literacy learning. There is a firm foundation that principals are key factors in overall student learning (Leithwood, Louis, Anderson, & Wahlstrom, 2004; Robinson, Lloyed, & Rowe, 2008). The learning process is either nurtured or starved through the actions or nonactions taken by school leaders. Principals who understand how to support teachers and students as they engage in learning are the difference between high impact and limited impact leadership in student learning.

Although there is a clear understanding that principals make a difference in student learning, little instruction is provided to principals in how to specifically scaffold the core technology of literacy learning in their buildings (Sulentic Dowell, Bickmore, & Hoewing, 2012). The book that follows is an important contribution in heightening principals' understanding of how to improve literacy learning in their schools. It examines the important principal leadership concepts of cultural, instructional, and managerial leadership in relationship to literacy and how those concepts are applied in schools. The authors weave these core principles together to magnify how best to scaffold teacher learning and practices related to literacy.

Of particular importance, this book invigorates—or perhaps reinvigorates—the principal's role in enhancing a healthy and positive culture in schools through the joyful experience of literacy learning for teachers and on behalf of students. As policy initiatives, such as No Child Left Behind and Race to the Top, gained prominence, principals' focus shifted. Out of necessity, principals' attention to test scores heightened while their attention to the joy of learning and authentic literacy experience seemed to slip.

This book contributes to the growing recognition that the pendulum needs to swing back. The evidence is deep that student emotions have impacts on learning and well-being (Durlak, Weissberg, Dymnicki, Taylor, & Schellinger, 2011). The evidence is also clear that teachers' emotions and well-being impact how they engage with and affect student learning (Sutton & Wheatley, 2003). The authors of this book clearly outline how principals can develop a culture of joy around literacy learning for and with teachers in the service of students.

The import of this book is clear: school leaders will learn how to better lead through melding core principal leadership concepts, effective components of literacy learning, and the development of practices that support teacher and student literacy engagement and learning. More importantly, this book will help principals accomplish all of this through enhancing a joyful culture centered on literacy.

—Dana L. Bickmore, Ph.D.
Program Coordinator and Associate Professor
Educational Policy and Leadership
University of Nevada Las Vegas

REFERENCES

Durlak, J. A., Weissberg, R. P., Dymnicki, A. B., Taylor, R. D., & Schellinger, K. B. (2011). The impact of enhancing students' social and emotional learning: A meta-analysis of school-based universal interventions. *Child Development, 82*(1), 405–432.

Leithwood, K. A., Louis, K. S., Anderson, S., & Wahlstrom, K. (2004). *How leadership influences student learning: Review of research.* Retrieved from Minneapolis; Toronto: www.wallacefoundation.org/SiteCollectionDocuments/WF/Knowledge%20Center/Attachments/PDF/ReviewofResearch-LearningFromLeadership.pdf

Robinson, V. M. J., Lloyed, C. A., & Rowe, K. (2008). The impact of leadership on student outcomes: An analysis of the differential effects of leadership types. *Educational Administration Quarterly, 44*(5), 635–674. doi:10.1177/0013161X08321509

Sulentic Dowell, M. M., Bickmore, D. L., & Hoewing, B. (2012). A framework for defining literacy leadership. *Journal of Reading Education, 37*(2), 7–15.

Sutton, R. E., & Wheatley, K. F. (2003). Teachers' emotions and teaching: A review of the literature and directions for future research. *Educational Psychology Review, 15*(4), 327–358.

Preface

The challenge for every literacy leader is to strike the right balance between making a necessary decision, accepting responsibility for that decision, and extending and agreeing to the autonomy granted to their teachers. In order to accomplish this balance, a literacy leader must recognize the needs of the faculty, acknowledge the varied levels of experience of the faculty, and identify how to structure and implement the right support frameworks to ensure that faculty are not left to struggle on their own in the name of autonomy. The purpose of this book is to provide elementary principals with concrete strategies to embrace the role of literacy leader.

To accomplish all this and serve the students, families, and school communities, literacy leaders need to meet the distinct needs of their teachers. Just as teachers are asked to meet the individual needs of their students, literacy leaders must understand that teachers have specific and different needs. Throughout this text, the authors explore autonomy and joy. Initiated, nurtured, and led by a literacy leader, the pairing of autonomy and joy has an exponential impact on teaching, learning, and student success.

Granting unrestricted autonomy to make instructional decisions seems to have a detrimental effect on experiencing joy in the classroom. In fact, unfettered autonomy seems to increase the stress levels of some teachers rather than to reduce stress. To address this, the authors posit intentional spaces for autonomy as well as differentiated approaches toward professional development.

Intentional autonomy takes into account a teacher's level of teaching experience, expertise in instructional decision-making, as well as a teacher's capacity to deliver high-quality literacy instruction. Like a delicate dance, literacy leaders must actively foster and support autonomy, but not be absent in their teachers' pursuit of instructional autonomy.

A literacy leader often acts as the buffer between the local, state, and federal mandates and their teachers. If teachers are to experience greater levels of joy in their classrooms as a result of autonomy, then they cannot be overburdened with policies that undermine their professional training and judgment. A literacy leader who is committed to creating joy through autonomy must defend his or her teachers from attacks on their professionalism. The attacks on professionalism can be hidden within intentional and unintentional teacher-shaming.

Teachers need literacy leaders who are advocates—who recognize that devoting time to family is as important to teachers as staying late or coming in early to work with students—literacy leaders who can assist them in growing as individuals and as professionals.

In order to expand teachers' feelings of joy, increase instructional autonomy, and address professionalism, the principal of a school must create an environment in which the culture of the school is honest and transparent. Reclaiming joy as a part of the teaching and learning experience is at the crux of this text. This book unpacks the ways a principal as literacy leader does this through research and vignettes.

Acknowledgments

TYNISHA

A heartfelt thank-you goes to my two daughters, Neenah and Nevaeh. I am blessed to have daughters who are patient with mom as she writes early in the morning or late into the night. I love you girls with all my heart. I am grateful to the Creator for every blessing and for putting the right people in my life at the right time.

I also wish to thank Margaret-Mary and Jason for embarking on this book venture. Jason, I am so grateful to you and your passion to be an excellent school leader who is honest, authentic, and vulnerable. I have learned so much from you as a person and as a leader. I am honored to call you my friend and colleague. Margaret-Mary, thank you for being a friend, mentor, and colleague. I value your honesty and support. You have been there through thick and thin. I am blessed to have you as a thought-partner and someone who is willing to help me think through all my ideas. I can't believe it, MM—we did it!

JASON

When I started in education over twenty years ago, I never would have dreamed of being a coauthor of a book. To think it's a book about literacy leadership seems even more surprising. I am so grateful for the surprising paths that life leads us down. I have been completely blessed to have had the support of so many people.

To my wife, Cathy, and daughters, Megan, Bayley, and Emily, thank you for being supportive and patient. Thank you for listening to my rants and believing in the work I do. Thanks for being the core reason I believe in public education and all that is good about it. To my coauthors, Margaret-Mary and Tynisha, I have never had the honor of learning so much from two superbly talented people. During every step of this journey, I remained in awe of your expertise. I am truly honored to have begun this process with colleagues and now end it with friends whom I will continue to call on for guidance and leadership. The teachers you both prepare for the profession should thank God every day for you being their instructors.

To the students and teachers at my elementary school, you are the reason for this book. It is for you and for everyone else who believes our teachers should be treated as professionals who deserve the trust to practice the instructional autonomy that is needed to meet the needs of their students. Special thanks to Tara Kempen, Jen Zurawski, Scott Marsden, and Dr. Amy LaPierre for putting up with my questioning. You four are the true experts who have helped me along this journey. To Shelly Drewiske, who always made sure I was writing and provided musical inspiration with her song choices when I got stuck.

Finally, it is with the deep gratitude that I recognize Lynne Mehlberg. Lynne served as my administrative assistant until she passed away after a long battle with breast cancer. She worked until three days before her death. She "got up, dressed up, and showed up" every day because she believed in Westwood. She was my biggest supporter. On the days I didn't believe in myself, she continued to believe in me. Every leader needs a support person who is not afraid to remind them that they are the boss. Lynne did this masterfully. Thank you, Lynne, for your support, mentoring, and believing in our mission. Miss you.

MARGARET-MARY

Thank you always to Tony, my husband and confidant. You continue to provide me with an example of what it means to be a true leader and to inspire me to lead from a mindset of service, a heart of gratitude, and to always be concerned about the good of all. I also wish to thank my children, Lilly and Adam, and my granddaughter, Zoe Anne, who have shared me with the world of education. I am indebted and grateful to Ty and Jason for this opportunity—it has been a grand journey—you are colleagues for life! Finally, I want to thank the many gifted, dedicated, and excellent elementary principals in the East Baton Rouge Parish School System and throughout south Louisiana whose fortitude, creativeness, vision, and excellence provide me with inspiration. I am especially indebted to Nakia Perkins and Earlisha Whitfield for what you have taught me about literacy leadership.

* * *

The authors want to also profusely thank Natalie Buhl. We could not have done this without your meticulous eye and quick turnaround. Thank you, Dr. Dana Bickmore, for taking time to write a forward; we are deeply grateful. Last but not least, thank you to Sarah Jubar, our acquisitions editor at Rowman & Littlefield, for all of your support and feedback.

Introduction

Maria is a third grade teacher in a suburban elementary school. She is in her sixth year of teaching. Although school starts at 8:30 a.m., Jason can count on her to be there by 7:15 each morning. Most days her car does not leave the parking lot until after 4:30 p.m. But her work doesn't end at 4:30 p.m. Most evenings are spent preparing for the next day, and weekends include preparing for the next week. Jason knows this because he is her building principal.

Jason also knows she loves teaching and her students. During weekly or bi-weekly walk-throughs, he notices her students gathered around her as she leads a read-aloud. Their eyes are focused on every word she reads. They sit on pins and needles waiting to find out what is going to happen next and they protest loudly when Maria states, "We'll have to wait until tomorrow to find out."

He witnesses her students engaged in their writing because she allows them choice of writing topic. In fact, when he stops and asks the students what they are writing, they politely share what they are working on, but he gets the sense they wish he would leave them alone and just let them write. The students are probably wondering, "Why is Dr. Lau taking me away from my writing? He is making me lose focus."

Each year Maria discovers an "unmotivated or disengaged reader." That same student in her class later becomes immersed in books and the literacy experience. The student is an active participant in the classroom community. Could Maria have magic fairy dust that she sprinkles on these students? Jason doubts it.

Maria knows how to build relationships and connect with her students. She invests time in getting to know each of them on a personal level. She goes beyond the prescribed literacy assessments used to inform instruction. She knows her students beyond the letter that identifies each of their reading levels. Maria has a deep understanding of students' home lives and interests. She has an overall sense of who her students are as living, breathing beings who will contribute to society in a productive way one day.

Unfortunately, Maria will say she is doing her students a disservice because she needs to "get through the content and complete all the assessments on time." As her principal, Jason knows she is doing her duty. She is following the prescribed curriculum, and she is turning in all assessment documents on time, so where is the problem?

Maria, who is one of Jason's best teachers, is exhausted. Her students are exhausted. She is exhausted because of the pace; she does not have the time to meet her students' instructional needs. She has to work doubly hard to fit in moments to differentiate, assess, teach, and continue to maintain strong relationships with each student. Where and how does Maria find joy?

Maria has been at this for six years. She is no longer a novice teacher. Jason has witnessed the significant gains of students because of her dedication, her knowledge of her craft, and her use of engaging pedagogical strategies. She is at her best when she is allowed to make decisions grounded in students' needs and in what she knows about effective literacy instruction. To be honest, Jason has a bias toward Maria. Jason hired her and visits her in her classroom at least once a week throughout the school year. She is a rock-star teacher. She is like the majority of teachers in Jason's school and in schools throughout the country.

Maria, like other teachers who entered into education, is committed to teaching her students to be creative, critical-thinking good citizens who are prepared to face the challenges of the next century. Maria entered the classroom as a wide-eyed, joyful, and enthusiastic teacher. She still is, but the unrealistic demands that are required in a seven-and-a-half-hour school day have become crushing. It is not the kids, the parents, or the administrators who take the enthusiasm or joy out of teaching—it is the burden of an overwhelming educational system.

Teachers like Maria find it hard to be at their best because of the pressures to get students to perform on standardized tests. For example, in a conversation with Maria, she stated to Jason,

> I think test scores create pressure. I think I am so worried about the test scores and moving kids forward that I am taking the joy out of learning for some kids. I am so concerned with the test. There's the pressure to be on this page on this lesson by Friday. And I'm not, so we need to just keep going.

Jason knows Maria is a dedicated teacher. He knows that she wants her students to do well. He knows that when Maria operates from a place of joy and passion, her students come alive. However, as he watches the Marias out there, he continues to grapple with the following questions:

- How many Marias are in the building?
- What is the principal's role as an instructional leader?
- What are the best ways to support teachers like Maria?
- What does a literacy leader do?
- What is the literacy leader's role in preventing teachers from becoming overwhelmed like Maria?

A NEW FOCUS: AUTONOMY AND JOY

In the era of standardized testing, educator effectiveness, and the highly politicized educational landscape, it may seem strange to write a book about teacher autonomy and joy. The authors argue this is the perfect time to focus on teacher autonomy and joy. There is enormous pressure on teachers to demonstrate student growth. Despite the pressure to achieve that goal, it seems they are becoming more restricted in the manner in which they choose to address the goal.

Every year teachers and administrators are bombarded with the latest and greatest packaged programs. Given the pressure they are under, teachers and administrators eagerly adopt these new programs to meet the needs of their students. Once the programs are adopted, teachers and administrators turn their focus to implementing the prepackaged program.

Checks by administrators and coaches are made during classroom walk-throughs and formal observations to make sure the materials from the purchased program are on display. District personnel want to ensure that dollars are well spent. Therefore, teachers must use the correct instructional language that is outlined in the teacher's manual and be on the appropriate page as outlined by the district-created scope and sequence. Their focus turns to program implementation rather than the instructional autonomy professional teachers bring to their students' growth and classroom culture.

Writing about joy, autonomy, and their impact on professionalism may seem fruitless. The authors beg to differ. It is exactly what we should talk about in education. According to Tim Walker (2016), a comparative education researcher who analyzes systems of education outside of the United States, we have a lot to learn from other nations. In fact, he notes that teachers need greater collective professional autonomy and more support to work with one another—in other words, more freedom from bureaucracy, but less from one another.

The work of Daniel Pink (2009) expresses the need for professionals (which includes teachers) to experience autonomy in their daily work so they can be more productive. Autonomy has been removed from the teaching profession resulting in the *de*professionalization of the profession and undermining the classroom teacher's ability to make the best instructional decisions to benefit students' knowledge construction, decision-making ability, and overall love of school and learning.

Teaching is a human endeavor, built on innate curiosity, creation, and collaborative spirit. But that is being removed from our classrooms. Instead of viewing students as children—most importantly as humans, with interests, feelings, and life experiences—the educational system forces teachers to view their students in terms of test scores and achievement rankings. While asked to focus on differentiating to meet the needs of their students, teachers are told to get through the content and make sure to be on section 3.2 of math by November 3.

If teachers focus on differentiation and the individual needs of their students, they run the risk of falling behind. Instead of being celebrated for differentiating and focusing on the needs of their students, teachers experience an overwhelming sense of pressure to get through the curriculum and a sense of failure if they are not as far along as their colleagues.

Unfortunately, the opposing messages result in teachers having to make a decision: Do they follow their professional instincts and do what is best for their students, or do they simply go through the motions of implementing the prepackaged instructional materials? It takes a great deal of confidence and skill to do the former rather than the latter. Unfortunately, we believe the system is designed to support the latter.

RECLAIMING JOY

A school that focuses on reclaiming teacher joy and autonomy is primarily focused on the needs of the students. A school not focused on teacher joy and autonomy cannot have students who are free to experience joy and autonomy in learning. To be clear, reclaiming teacher joy and autonomy does *not* mean there is an absence of standards, curricular framework, or assessment. These three things set the foundation to assist in the creation of autonomy and joy. But perhaps more importantly, school climate must be positive, inclusive, and welcoming.

Recent research suggests that a happy school can help students succeed regardless of the socioeconomic status of the students (Lonsdorf, 2016). In order to have a positive school climate, a school must value students as well as teachers, who are directly responsible for delivering content. To rebuild a *de*professionalized profession, community members and administrators must create a climate in which teachers are trusted to make informed instructional decisions for their students in spite of mandated curricular programs.

A culture of trust within a school begins collaboratively between teachers and administrators and evolves into a culture in which teachers trust their individual judgment. It includes an open dialogue between teachers and administrators. For administrators, building trust means listening to their teachers. Principals need to hear what their teachers are saying and feeling. This helps principals in the decision-making process know how much to support the current efforts of the teachers and how much to push the teachers to keep their current efforts moving forward. In order to navigate this landscape, principals must seek to develop relational trust.

Bryk and Schneider (2003) help us to understand the power of trust, particularly within the context of reform. We use the same framework within the context of building autonomy.

- Most teachers work hard at their teaching.
- Teachers must assume risks.
- Teachers deal with organizational conflict.
- Teacher should attempt new practices.
- Teachers must engage with colleagues in planning, implementing, and evaluating improvement initiatives.

Having trust also means trusting that teachers have the knowledge and skills to make instructional decisions without the fear of being vilified when their decisions fail. Many educators express a desire for autonomy in their decision-making. They express a desire to be free of the rigid requirements set forth by district-level decisions or the prescribed prepackaged instructional programs that promise to close the achievement gap.

However, while there is a strong desire for autonomy, administrators send conflicting messages of autonomy. The schedule is preassigned, the allotted minutes for instruction are given, and nonnegotiables are developed. While frameworks are necessary, a strict framework significantly reduces the level of autonomy teachers have to make the appropriate instructional decisions in their classroom.

As autonomy for teachers has shrunk over the years, the deprofessionalization of teaching has increased. This is highlighted by recent policy changes that have continued to whittle away at the professional skills of teachers. The rise in alternative, fast-tracked teacher-preparation programs has created a system in which the teaching profession is viewed as a set of skills that is easily acquired.

"When a job is treated as a profession, employment is grounded in a deep body of knowledge and set of skills. There are no alternative routes to medicine, and such routes to law are almost non-existent. In many ways, the profession of teaching has never reached the level of medicine or law, but throughout the past five or six decades it did rise to a genuine profession" (Mathis & Wellner, 2015, p. 2). Very few people would consider seeking medical treatment from a doctor who took a six-week course in medicine. However, it seems policy-makers are comfortable in a crash course for teachers who are tasked with laying the groundwork in the classroom for our future doctors.

Other threats to the profession are the evaluation practices based on student test scores that result in the adoption of scripted and narrow curriculums. These policies do not seem to match the majority of Americans (62 percent) who have confidence in the public school system. Additionally, 63 percent of the American public oppose using test scores as a means of teacher evaluation (Mathis & Wellner, 2015). If this is the case, then why do policy-makers insist on marginalizing teachers and work to undermine the profession?

To wait for policy-makers to see the need to adopt policy change is fruitless. If teachers and administrators have a desire to reclaim joy and autonomy in their classrooms and schools, then they must recommit to the profession they have chosen and show the power of joy and autonomy. The first step to reclaiming joy is to establish, or rebuild, a school culture that puts the needs of students and teachers at the core.

While school culture is collaborative, the onus of creating a successful school culture falls on the shoulders of the building principal. A successful school culture that is grounded in the shared beliefs of the staff is imperative to the school's ability to flourish when meeting the needs of its students (Habegger, 2008). School culture is deeper than staff who like each other, students who get along, and parents who like their child's school. A strong school culture includes all of those things but also becomes a living and breathing entity that focuses on continual improvement.

A strong school culture is one in which teachers are willing to be vulnerable when teaching. It includes principals who are willing to support their teachers' risk-taking regardless of success or failure. It also is a culture in which students are viewed as active participants in the learning process. They are allowed choice in their learning. Without a strong school culture, teachers will never experience joy and autonomy in their classrooms.

CHAPTER OVERVIEW

The purpose of this book is to support elementary literacy leaders—more specifically building principals—in supporting teachers to reclaim joy, understand the power of having a clear vision for literacy instruction, and ultimately take their place as true literacy leaders who can work in tandem with literacy coaches and other support staff to increase student achievement when accountability looms over all of us. Each coauthor contributes to this text from his or her own point of view as a literacy leader. Their combined experiences include being a building principal, assistant superintendent, director of pupil services, and co-founder of a charter school.

Chapter 1 sets the foundation for the text as well as the relationship between literacy leadership and joy in teaching. The chapter focuses on principal literacy knowledge and why it matters. The authors grappled with the location of this chapter, but this chapter sets the tone and provides readers with a common language that will be used throughout this book. This chapter also gives a definition of *joy* and provides the framework for why it matters and why it has value in today's schools. For literacy leaders, there is an urgent need for literacy knowledge. The chapter will outline key tenets of literacy knowledge needed for a literacy leader to be effective. The authors recognize that as a building principal in an elementary school, you are a literacy leader, a cultural leader, and an instructional leader. They are different roles, but three hats that must be worn well.

Chapter 2 takes a deep dive into belief statements. Organizational leaders will agree that effective leaders have a vision and can communicate the vision to key stakeholders. This chapter supports building principals in creating a belief statement that serves as the vision for instruction. The authors provide examples of and suggestions for how to infuse joy and autonomy into the culture of the building. Belief statements are one way to keep the vision at the forefront of decision-making.

Chapter 3 is all about joy. Need we say more?

Chapter 4 focuses on autonomy and trust. Teachers must be partners in the work of educating students. As literacy leaders, they do the work. Principals are facilitators. There is a concerted focus on why teacher autonomy matters and concrete ways in which principals can begin the process of building trust among their elementary teachers.

Chapter 5, unlike the other chapters, is focused on supporting teachers in seeing themselves as professionals. The authors' goal is for principals to be allies for their teachers rather than opponents.

Chapter 6 is all about culture and climate. This chapter is intended to push thinking about school culture beyond the "happy hour."

Chapter 7 is a call-to-action chapter. In order to shift culture, teachers must own their development. The chapter focuses on how to give teachers autonomy through the use of professional development communities (PDCs).

Chapter 8 takes a specific focus on literacy culture. Elementary schools must have more than the literacy coach and classroom teachers engaged in literacy learning. This chapter shifts to literacy permeating the building and ways to encourage the whole school community to adopt a literacy culture.

Chapter 9 shifts to the day-to-day interactions principals have, such as walk-throughs and teacher evaluations. The chapter focuses on how to give feedback, specifically in the area of literacy instruction, that encourages teacher growth as well as student growth. This chapter also turns the mirror back on the literacy leader as part of the humanistic process of teaching. This chapter challenges you to look forward.

Each chapter also includes reflective questions for you as the reader to use as you see fit.

The authors recognize that this is a journey. They will share their wins and pitfalls. The vignettes included within each chapter are their way of inviting you into the process and the conversation we continue to have as literacy leaders.

REFERENCES

Bryk, A. S., & Schneider, B. (2003). Trust in schools: A core resource for school reform. *Educational Leadership, 60*(6), 40–45.

Habegger, S. (2008). The principal's role in successful schools: Creating a positive school culture. *Principal, 88*(1), 44–46.

Lonsdorf, K. (2016). How a happy school can help students succeed. *National Public Radio.* Retrieved from www.npr.org/sections/ed/2016/11/01/500060004/how-a-happy-school-can-help-students-succeed

Mathis, W., & Wellner, K. (2015). Research-based options for education policymaking reversing the deprofessionalization of teaching. *National Education Policy Center.* Retrieved from http://greatlakescenter.org/docs/Policy_Briefs/Research-Based-Options-2015/02-Mathis-Welner-Deprofessionalization.pdf

Pink, D. (2009). *Drive: The surprising truth about what motivates us.* New York, NY: Riverhead.

Walker, T. (2016). Teacher autonomy declined over past decade, new data shows. *NEA Today.* Retrieved from http://neatoday.org/2016/01/11/teacher-autonomy-in-the-classroom

Chapter One

The Connections between Literacy Leadership and Joy in Teaching

There is no magic bullet, preferred sequence, special materials, prescribed scope and sequence, or best way to lead teachers. While leadership styles abound, the role of a literacy leader is complex—it encompasses relationship skills, content and pedagogical knowledge, expertise with organizational management, supervision ability, competence at evaluation, and working in collaboration with teachers, students, families, and communities.

EDUCATIONAL LEADERSHIP

By tradition and convention in the United States, being a principal and enacting educational leadership includes a multitude of managerial tasks and leadership skills, all focused on supporting student learning (Hallinger & Snidvongs, 2008). While management of the day-to-day operation of the school is a significant aspect of the leadership and management of a school campus, principal leadership skills extend beyond management tasks. The instructional leadership provided to all school stakeholders is instrumental to improving student outcomes (Leithwood, Louis, Anderson, & Wahlstrom, 2004). Within the body of educational leadership literature that exists, researchers have framed in theory the complexities of effective principal leadership in specific ways.

The most prominent theories have been *instructional* and *transformational* leadership theories (Leithwood et al., 2004; Printy, Marks, & Bowers, 2009; Robinson, Lloyed, & Rowe, 2008). The key issue between these two theories is the question of whether principals should be more directly involved in the curriculum and instructional practices of teachers and orches-

1

trate school and teacher improvement *or* whether principals lead through building collective capacity and commitment to shared organizational goals. The theory of instructional leadership advocates building individual teacher capacity while the transformational theory of leadership recommends developing organizational capacity (Marks & Printy, 2003; Robinson, Lloyed, & Rowe, 2008).

In particular, Printy, Marks, and Bowers (2009) describe instructional leadership as "oriented toward improvement of instructional, curricular, and assessment practices to improve pedagogical quality and raise student achievement" (p. 507). Like other educational researchers, the authors suggest that a combination of leadership styles is necessary for effective school leadership (Hallinger, 2003; Hallinger & Heck, 2009; Leithwood et al., 2004; Marks & Printy, 2003; Printy, Marks, & Bowers, 2009).

Of note to all who read this text and to those who are interested in educational leadership styles is the work of Robinson, Lloyed, and Rowe (2008), who, in their seminal meta-analysis of the interplay between principal leadership and student outcomes, specified that "the comparison between instructional and transformational leadership showed that the impact of the former is three to four times that of the latter" (p. 665).

ABOUT THE AUTHORS

As the authors and as educational leaders who have experience at the school level, the district level, and the collegiate level, the authors clearly recognize that leadership committed to organizational goals and focused on organizational changes is imperative for student success. One style of leadership may be inadequate for ideal student development. As educators and scholars, the authors contend that leadership that develops teacher instructional capacity as well as leadership that fosters and maintains a culture where teachers feel they collaboratively have an impact on students is instrumental in improving student outcomes.

Although she has never been a school principal, Tynisha served in several administrative and instructional support roles for Teach for America's (TFA) summer institute. She was a TFA corps member from 2002 to 2004, teaching in both the Rio Grande Valley in Texas and in the Baltimore City Public Schools in Maryland. Because of her experiences, she decided to focus her career goals on teaching and teacher preparation. As a school director, curriculum coordinator, and curriculum specialist for TFA, Tynisha's signature focus was the need for a depth of literacy knowledge as well as leadership capacity, which she sees as integral to supporting novice teachers as well as facilitators. She has functioned as the co-chair of teacher education at her liberal arts institution since 2009.

Margaret-Mary came to educational leadership through a circular route. A career educator with fifteen years of teaching experience, which includes initial National Board Certification in 1995, as she moved from the school level to a district perspective, she recognized the keen need for literacy leadership. As the assistant superintendent of sixty-four elementary schools for a large, urban district in Louisiana from 2002 to 2006, her leadership amid the displacement and turmoil of Hurricane Katrina was both instructional and transformational (Sulentic Dowell, 2008, 2012).

While administrative work consumes most educational leaders and could have taken priority in terms of a personal career trajectory, the lives and well-being of children, teachers, and their families were Margaret-Mary's priority. She left administration for higher education, where she coordinates her university's Grade 1–5 Teacher Education Program.

Jason began his career in education as a school psychologist for a larger urban school district and then served as a school psychologist in a small, affluent district. It was during his time in the smaller district that he was encouraged to seek an administrative position. He later became director of pupil services for the district. In 2002, he became the director of student services for his current school district. He never considered being a principal, but having worked with talented principals throughout his career, he responded to the call to seek out a building leadership position. Fortunately, that opportunity happened within his school district at his children's elementary school. It was during a review of data that he became passionate about literacy for his elementary students.

Jason is committed to leading his building through a process of improving the literacy levels of his students by focusing on three reading beliefs:

1. Student choice and easy access to books influence motivation and achievement.
2. Time should be made for read-alouds and independent reading on a regular basis.
3. Positive relationships and connections can be built through reading.

These reading beliefs have served as his guide, and the school's guide, when making instructional decisions related to literacy. Finally, his secondary passion is to help his teachers and students experience autonomy and joy in their teaching and learning. Without the presence of autonomy and joy, he believes the passion for learning and student achievement cannot be cultivated.

Tynisha, Margaret-Mary, and Jason each took a different path to literacy and teaching, and each has distinctive experience in terms of leadership. However, their interests converge at the intersectionality of literacy and leadership and connect them as educators, researchers, and scholars.

For example, Margaret-Mary and Tynisha, in collaboration with others, founded the District Level Literacy Leadership (DiLL) Special Interest Group (SIG) for the International Literacy Association (ILA), where the focus is creating a space for principals, coaches, curriculum directors, and others in pivotal roles to engage in dialogue, ideation, and solution generation specific to literacy. Margaret-Mary, in collaboration with others, continues to be an influential scholar in the emerging field of literacy leadership. Tynisha and Jason have been active by engaging practitioners and providing concrete solutions to support literacy leaders at a regional level and in practitioner-based publications such as *Literacy Today*, a publication of the ILA.

INSTRUCTIONAL LEADERSHIP

Instructional leadership, as delineated by Hallinger (2003), Hallinger and Heck (1996, 1998), Hallinger and Murphy (1985), and Zepeda (2007), and perhaps the most researched model of instructional leadership reported in the field of educational leadership literature, contends that the principal's multifaceted duties include the following:

1. leading the development and support of a school mission,
2. managing the instructional program, and
3. developing a positive school culture.

Although the principal is a central position within a school campus, Hallinger (2003) clearly suggests that the accomplishment of these three primary instructional leadership tasks requires shared and collaborative actions between the principal and teachers, which contributes to a positive school culture.

It is important to note that Hallinger and associates' framework of instructional leadership also aligns with national U.S. standards of instructional leadership, including the *Interstate School Leaders Licensure Consortium* (ISLLC) standards (Council of Chief State School Officers, 2008) and the standards promoted by the National Association of Elementary School Principals (NAESP) (2001). In particular, in the NAESP publication, *Standards for What Principals Should Know and Be Able to Do* (2001), both standards 3 and 4 benchmark the instructional leadership role of elementary principals. These standards also reveal how principals must balance management and instructional leadership roles, while promoting, nurturing, and guiding a culture for adult learning within a school faculty. In conclusion, the theory of instructional leadership is reinforced by these leadership standards and maintained by the research from which the standards were developed.

The following vignette illustrates the complex issues that surround the principalship and the myriad responsibilities that pull at elementary principals each day.

Waking up every day with the intent to make a difference in the lives of children, you don't think about what your role is as just an instructional leader or the title given to you by a committee. You start each day with the intent to make a difference, change a life, or help someone to improve. Every morning on my ride to work, there is no time to listen to the radio or enjoy the morning drive. I ride in silence, as I'm constantly thinking of ways to create, improve, achieve, sustain, motivate, and impact a child's life. Every morning I reflect on two questions, "What will you have me to do?" and "What would you have me to say?" (Williamson, 2008), and I work from that space.

Once I've entered the building, which is usually alone, and most times as the first person to arrive, I organize and prepare for the day according to the calendar reminders that are waiting for me on my computer monitor. I sketch out a daily plan/map according to each day's priorities and this question: "What is in the best interest of students today?" I schedule myself for specific, daily grade-level vertical planning meetings, grade-level meetings, professional learning community meetings, classroom observations, and classroom walk-throughs.

Out of need, I also prepare for impromptu happenings such as parking lot and outdoor visits, custodial briefings, parent visits, parent conference calls, teacher drop-ins, weekly finance meetings with the secretary, before- and after-school duty, lunch duty, and a call or visit at any given moment from the school executive director or the district superintendent. In between, before, and after these daily events, I must meet with the instructional leadership team, teacher leaders, and sometimes with just the assistant principal to ensure that the procedures, routines, plans, schedules, programs, initiatives, and strategies are in place and running smoothly.

As my day comes to an end, which is usually by evening, I mentally begin to prepare all over again for the next day. As I drive home, there is usually no time to stop for an errand or listen to the radio and enjoy the evening ride home, but rather a habitual act of replaying the entire day of events while thinking of the things that were possibly forgotten, overlooked, not discussed, or simply not finished, all while continuing to focus on imminent planning that will support improving and sustaining student achievement. (Nakia Perkins, Elementary Principal)

As Nakia's vignette illustrates, the roles and responsibilities of an elementary principal are demanding. Literacy leadership is a dimension of leadership that an elementary principal considers each day as she confronts what each day brings, looking at immediate goals and concerns and planning for the long-term, reflecting, reevaluating, and reestablishing priorities.

DEFINING LITERACY LEADERSHIP: WHAT IT ENTAILS, WHAT IT LOOKS LIKE

According to the National Policy Board for Educational Administration: Professional Standards for Educational Leaders (NPBEA), formerly ISLLCS, "The growing knowledge and the challenging demands of the job [the principalship] require educational leaders to guide their practice in directions that will be most beneficial to students" (NPBEA, 2015, p. 1).

Outlining the foundational principles of leadership, the school principal as the educational leader should be able to exert influence on student achievement by creating challenging, but caring and supportive, conditions conducive to each student's learning, to relentlessly develop and support teachers, to create positive working conditions, to effectively allocate resources, to construct appropriate organizational policies and systems, and to engage in other deep and meaningful work outside of the classroom that has a powerful impact on what happens inside of the classroom (NPBEA, 2015, p. 1).

Literacy leadership is a prime example of this notion of "the growing knowledge and the challenging demands of the job" so aptly described by the NPBEA (2015, p. 1). As literacy research expands, so, then, does the knowledge base needed for literacy leadership, whether it be content about literacy, recommended literacy practices, or how teachers, principals, and schools promote and maintain literacy practices that result in increased student achievement.

LITERACY LEADERSHIP

Part art and part science, literacy leadership—leading teachers in regard to literacy efforts that result in increased student outcomes—involves acquired pedagogical skill sets and content knowledge, combined with the ability to deliver that knowledge and skill, as well as the relational skills required to support teachers. Literacy leadership also includes the ability to enact a literacy mission and vision that guides the teachers, staff, students, and families connected to a campus. This is the rallying point for why literacy matters and the role literacy will have as an integral part of school culture.

Creating a professional community among faculty and staff is a vital aspect of literacy leadership (Booth & Rowsell, 2007). The literacy leader is typically perceived as the *instructional leader* of a school campus (Bickmore & Sulentic Dowell, 2011; Sulentic Dowell, Hoewing, & Bickmore, 2012).

While instructional leadership is an established, recognized, and acknowledged traditional leadership exemplar in schooling in the United States and enjoys an established and rich tradition (Criscuolo, 1984; Donmoyer & Wagstaff, 1990; Hallinger, 2003; Leithwood et al., 2004; Robinson, Lloyed, & Rowe, 2008), literacy leadership is a growing field (Booth & Rowsell, 2007; Criscuolo, 1984; Hoewing & Sulentic Dowell, 2010; Matsumura, Sartoris, DiPrima Bickel, & Garnier, 2009; McKenna & Walpole, 2008; Protheroe, 2008; Reeves, 2008; Sulentic Dowell, Hoewing, & Bickmore, 2012; Tooms, 2003).

In short, literacy leadership can be viewed as a subset of instructional leadership that converges to support student learning (Hallinger & Snidvongs, 2008). Evidence suggests principals who engage in establishing a literacy agenda, who support teachers' professional and teaching development in the area of literacy, and who possess the expertise to provide access to literacy resources and build organizational capacity for literacy growth positively impact students' literacy development (Booth & Rowsell, 2007). Literacy leaders must demonstrate what they expect.

Two major areas of knowledge converge to define the elementary principal as literacy leader—content knowledge and pedagogical knowledge. While important at all levels, literacy leadership is essential at the elementary level (Allen, 2016; Booth & Rowsell, 2007; McKenna & Walpole, 2008; Neuman, 2009). An elementary principal's understanding of the complexity of literacy processes involves both pools of knowledge.

Content knowledge (Booth & Rowsell, 2007; Cummins, 2006; Halliday, 1973; Kucer, 2001; Stein & Nelson, 2003) is what constitutes the essentials of listening, speaking, reading, and writing, and the cognitive processes that contribute to literacy. Content knowledge also constitutes the skill sets needed to establish, nurture, and maintain a school culture and a working knowledge of children's literature that supports students' literacy learning and growth (Booth & Rowsell, 2007).

An elementary principal also needs to understand recommended pedagogical practice spanning developmental age ranges, typically kindergarten through fifth or sixth grade, depending on a school's grade-level configurations, and discipline-specific content from social studies, science, math, and physical education (Cunningham & Allington, 2007; Prince & Conaway, 1985; Rasinski, 2003; Stein & Nelson, 2003). Providing school configurations to support literacy (Reeves, 2008), or what Booth and Rowsell (2007) term "learning time and space" (p. 31), is also part of literacy content knowledge.

For example, essential content knowledge for elementary principals is the importance of access to literature, especially for children who lack opportunity to access literature in homes and communities, and how to facilitate access to print through classroom libraries, school libraries, and access through digital formats. Additional aspects of literacy content knowledge include principals at the elementary level needing adequate background about literacy in order to mediate the difference between and among commercial programs and differing approaches, including assessments (Booth & Rowsell, 2007).

For instance, it's important for elementary principals to know the research basis for the Reading Recovery program (Clay, 1987), the writing process (Murray, 2003), and reading and writing workshop formats (Adams, 2004; Graves, 1994), as well as the diagnostic accuracy and the psychology-based theory behind common assessments such as the Dynamic Indicators of Basic Early Literacy (DIBELS) (Good & Kaminski, 2002). Layered on top of this requisite knowledge is how an elementary principal negotiates the issues of competing instructional models such as balanced literacy (Burns, 2006) or a skill-based approach and how to finesse supervising the delivery of a district-mandated or state-mandated curriculum (Booth & Rowsell, 2007). Literacy content knowledge (see table 1.1), then, also equates to elementary principals who function as literacy leaders to know and understand both seminal and current literacy research.

Pedagogical knowledge of instructional strategies used by great teachers, master educators, and coaches is also essential knowledge for elementary principals to acquire. As an example, elementary principals need to know the pedagogical significance of establishing literacy routines, the importance of setting up daily reading and writing time, and the efficacy of teachers creating flexible grouping strategies for literacy instruction and practice (Cantrell, 1999; McKenna & Walpole, 2008). While a deep understanding of this knowledge is imperative, elementary principals simultaneously need to acquire the skills required to supervise, lead, and evaluate literacy teaching, coaching, and learning (Booth & Rowsell, 2007; Reeves, 2008).

And, while the fields of educational leadership and literacy leadership can define what it means to be an effective leader based on theoretical models and knowledge constructs, great teaching is harder to define and operationalize. While no formula exists for what constitutes a great teacher, great teaching is tangible and recognizable.

Elementary principals recognize that teaching stems from relationships that are cultivated with students, the ability to know students, assess their strengths and weaknesses, and plan accordingly, implementing both content and pedagogical skill. Good teachers, those who know their discipline and craft, teach with ease. Great teachers demand excellence by their craft and experience joy in teaching well. However, in the last several decades, political and commercial interests and pressures have exacerbated the roles and responsibilities of elementary principals and of elementary teachers.

Table 1.1. Literacy Knowledge Table

Theme	Code Categories	Codes	Code Frequency
Understanding the Complexity of Literacy Processes	Content knowledge (819 instances)	Oral language development	47
		Print awareness	38
		Linguistic Knowledge	23
		Phonemic Awareness	62
		Phonics	78
		Decoding	68
		Fluency	79
		Vocabulary	86
		Cognition; complex thinking	60
		Comprehension	123
		Narrative and expository literature	28
		Composition (spelling and writing)	77
		Functions of language	21
		Personal-sociocultural aspects	29
	Knowledge of best practice spanning developmental age ranges and content areas (385 instances)	Instruction based on assessment	77
		Daily reading and writing practice	88
		Age and developmentally appropriate reading material	33
		Reading aloud	42
		Reading and writing co-development	37
		Flexible groupings	65
		Reading and writing processes	43

Theme	Code Categories	Codes	Code Frequency
	Provide school structures to support literacy (163 instances)	Access to print/ literature	76
		Provision for literacy instruction and learning	48
		Organizing classrooms for optimal learning	39
Instructional Strategies Used by Master Educators and Coaches	Literacy environment and management systems (241 instances)	Assessing literacy formally and informally	31
		Flexible skill grouping	68
		Teacher/child interactions	21
		Establishing routines	57
		Teaching at instructional level	13
		Mix of whole- and small-group teaching	51
Supervision to Promote High- Quality Literacy Instruction	Monitoring and evaluation of literacy instruction (436 instances)	Establishing relationships	61
		Support teachers and coaches	97
		Evaluate teachers and coaches	103
		Professional development	111
		Classroom environment	64

Source: M-M. Sulentic Dowell, B. Hoewing, & D. Bickmore. (2012). A framework for defining literacy leadership. *Journal of Reading Education, 37*(2), 7–15. Published with permission.

COMMODIFICATION OF U.S. EDUCATION

As if the demands of literacy leadership such as content knowledge, peda-gogical awareness, management expertise, and supervision skill were not complex and time-consuming in themselves, there are other pressures faced by a literacy leader that impact the degree to which principals feel successful and teachers feel empowered. Empowerment and job satisfaction in a people-oriented profession such as teaching leads to joy. However, shifts in legislation and accountability, a direct result of the commodification of education, and the politics of literacy (Bomer, 2005) have all but changed both the description and the perception of the role of a principal in many states in the United States.

Complicated commercial and powerful political forces confront public education in the twenty-first century (Schneider, 2014, 2015, 2016). It is convenient for corporate interests to want to demonize public education in the United States (Berliner & Glass, 2014). The commodification and corporatization of education requires that elementary principals who are literacy leaders assume a dynamic standpoint in improving teacher quality. Understanding the political interests in literacy, policy shifts, and the commercialization of literacy teaching and learning was spurred by passage of the No Child Left Behind (NCLB) (2001) and the Every Student Succeeds Act (ESSA) (2016).

While ESEA was focused on education as a means of addressing economic inequities, NCLB and ESSA have resulted in a narrow-minded fascination with accountability in the form of formulaic, packaged, scripted curricula and high-stakes tests that have effectively silenced teacher voices and have stifled creativity (Allington, 2002a, 2002b, 2005; Altwerger, 2005; Garan, 2002, 2004; Coles, 2003; Johnson & Johnson, 2002; Johnson, Johnson, Ness, & Farenga, 2008). This myopic focus on standardized testing and the resultant impact on teaching has stripped teachers of the joy that occurs when teachers connect with students during literacy teaching and the personal excitement and satisfaction teachers experience when children make literacy learning connections (Gallagher, 2009; Garan, 2002).

Within the past two decades, commercial and political forces have escalated (Allington, 2004; Garan, 2002), determining the kind of instruction public school children, specifically elementary children, receive, narrowing curriculum and teaching to what content is presented by a state high-stakes test. Johnson and Johnson (2002) push back against this commodification and politicization of literacy, claiming that eliminating the U.S. "achievement gap" cannot be realized unless equity in schools, homes, and communities is addressed.

Escalating mandates derived from NCLB (2001) and ESSA (2016) legislation, crafted as accountability, have dictated how educators teach. Frequently the literacy mandated for elementary children, especially public school children who are poor, urban, and rural, and children of color, fails to foster creativity (Finn, 1999). As an example, in elementary schools, social studies and science have been de-emphasized within the last two decades, solely because they are not tested subjects. An astounding 71 percent of America's school districts have reduced arts, science, and social studies in-

structional minutes for increased time on the high-stakes subjects—specifically the English Language Arts (The Center on Education Policy, 2006).

Accountability formulas and the pressure from politics have also focused
unwarranted attention on teachers and public schools in the United States.
And as the pressures from politics, commercial interests, and public policy
intensify, public schools get blamed for poverty with the erroneous expectation that, somehow, schools can mitigate the social issues that arise when
children from impoverished backgrounds do not achieve at the same rate as
wealthier peers (Apple, 2012; Berliner & Glass, 2014; Finn, 2010). Teachers
get blamed for poverty.

And the success of a school is now directly tied to the role of the principal. According to the Professional Standards for Educational Leaders:
NPBEA, the principal, or educational leader, must be ready to effectively
meet the challenges and opportunities of the job today and in the future as
education, schools, and society continue to shift (NPBEA, 2015).

This chapter highlights the connections between what a literacy leader
achieves within his or her campus as an instructional literacy leader to encourage, promote, and support teachers, and the subsequent response by
teachers to administrative leadership expectations to teach with capacity,
with expertise, and with confidence. In a time when many teachers feel
disenfranchised and devalued and express a loss of joy in their chosen profession, literacy leadership can serve to empower teachers to teach with
authority, confidence, and conviction, which, in turn, equates to inspiring
students to learn.

Chapter 2 begins to delve deep into the concrete ways literacy leaders can
influence and change their school culture to embrace literacy development.
Belief statements are explored as part of the vision-setting process.

REFLECTION QUESTIONS

- Why is it necessary for elementary school principals to possess literacy
  knowledge?
- What is your literacy mission and vision for your school?
- How would you rate your literacy content knowledge and your literacy
  pedagogical knowledge on a scale of 1 (low) to 5 (high)?
- How have you "owned" your own development as a literacy leader to
  build your literacy content knowledge and your literacy pedagogical
  knowledge?
- How would you describe your role as the instructional leader of your
  school/campus?
- What is your current knowledge about the politics of literacy and the
  commodification of education?

REFERENCES

Adams, A. S. (2004). *How to make writing curriculum decisions based on the assessment of students' needs* (Unpublished master's thesis). California State University, San Marcos, CA.

Allen, J. (2016). *Becoming a literacy leader: Supporting learning and change.* Portland, ME: Stenhouse.

Allington, R. (2002a). *Big brother and the national reading curriculum: How ideology trumped evidence.* Portsmouth, NH: Heinemann.

Allington, R. (2002b). What I've learned about effective reading instruction from a decade of studying exemplary elementary classroom teachers. *Phi Delta Kappan, 83,* 740–747.

Allington, R. (2004, March). Setting the record straight. *Educational Leadership, 61,* 22–25.

Allington, R. (2005, October–November). NCLB, reading first and whither the future? *Reading Today,* 18.

Altwerger, B. (2005). *Reading for profit.* Portsmouth, NH: Heinemann.

Apple, M. W. (2012). *Education and power.* New York, NY: Routledge.

Berliner, D. C., & Glass, G. V. (Eds.). (2014). *50 myths and lies that threaten America's public schools: The real crisis in education.* New York, NY: Teachers College Press.

Bickmore, D. L., & Sulentic Dowell, M-M. (2011). Concerns, use of time, and the intersections of leadership: Case study of two charter school principals. *Research in the schools, 18*(1), 44–61.

Bomer, R. (2005). Missing the children: When politics and programs impede our teaching. *Language Arts, 82,* 168–176.

Booth, D., & Rowsell, J. (2007). *The literacy principal, leading, supporting, and assessing reading and writing initiatives* (2nd ed.). Markham, Ontario: Pembroke Publishers.

Burns, B. (2006). *How to teach balanced reading and writing.* Thousand Oaks, CA: Corwin Press.

Cantrell, S. (1999). Effective teaching and literacy learning: A look inside primary classrooms. *The Reading Teacher, 52,* 370–378.

The Center on Education Policy. (2006). *From the capital to the classroom: Year 4 of the No Child Left Behind Act.* Washington, DC: Author.

Clay, M. (1987). Implementing Reading Recovery: Systemic adaptations to an educational innovation. *New Zealand Journal of Educational Studies, 22*(1), 35–58.

Coles, G. (2003). *Reading: The naked truth.* Portsmouth, NH: Heinemann.

Council of Chief State School Officers. (2008). Educational leadership policy standards: ISLLC 2008. Retrieved from www.wallacefoundation.org/SiteCollectionDocuments/WF/Knowledge%20Center/Attachments/PDF/ISLLC%202008.pdf

Criscuolo, N. (1984). A reading checklist. *The School Administrator, 41*(2), 20–21.

Cummins, C. (2006). *Understanding Reading First initiatives.* Newark, DE: International Reading Association.

Cunningham, P., & Allington, R. (2007). *Classrooms that work* (4th ed.). Boston, MA: Pearson.

Donmoyer, R., & Wagstaff, J. (1990). Principals can be effective managers and instructional leaders. *NASSP Bulletin, 74*(525), 20–29.

Every Student Succeeds Act. (2016). *Public Law No. 114-95.* One hundred fourteenth Congress of the United States of America.

Finn, P. (1999). *Literacy with an attitude.* Albany, NY: State University of NY Press.

Finn, P. J. (2010). *Literacy with an attitude: Educating working-class children in their own self-interest.* Albany, NY: State University of New York Press.

Gallagher, K. (2009). *Readicide.* Portland, ME: Stenhouse.

Garan, E. (2002). *Resisting reading mandates.* Portsmouth, NH: Heinemann.

Garan, E. (2004). *In defense of our children.* Portsmouth, NH: Heinemann.

Good, R. H., & Kaminski, R. (2002) Dynamic Indicators of Basic Early Literacy Skills. Retrieved from https://dibels.org/html

Graves, D. H. (1994). *A fresh look at writing.* Portsmouth, NH: Heinemann.

Halliday, M. (1973). *Explorations in the functions of language.* London, UK: Edward Arnold.

Hallinger, P. (2011). A review of three decades of doctoral studies using the Principal Instructional Management Rating Scale: A lens on methodological progress in educational leadership. *Educational Administration Quarterly, 47*(2), 271–306. doi: 10.1177/0013161X10383412

Hallinger, P., & Heck, R. H. (1996). Reassessing the principal's role in school effectiveness: A review of empirical research, 1980–1995. *Educational Administration Quarterly, 32*(1), 5–44. doi: 10.1177/0013161X96032001002

Hallinger, P., & Heck, R. H. (1998). Exploring the principal's contribution to school effectiveness: 1980–1995. *School Effectiveness and School Improvement, 9*(2), 157–191. doi: 10.1080/0924345980090203

Hallinger, P., & Heck, R. H. (2009). Distributed leadership in schools: Does system policy make a difference? In A. Harris (Ed.), *Distributed leadership: Different perspectives* (pp. 101–117). Dordrecht: Springer Netherlands.

Hallinger, P., & Murphy, J. (1985). Assessing the instructional management behavior of principals. *Elementary School Journal, 86*(2), 217–247.

Hallinger, P., & Snidvongs, K. (2008). Educating leaders: Is there anything to learn from business management? *Educational Management Administration & Leadership, 36*(1), 9–31. doi: 10.1177/1741143207084058

Hoewing, B., & Sulentic Dowell, M-M. (2010). The elementary principal as chief literacy officer: Myth, legend, fairy tale or reality? *Journal of the Southern Regional Council of Educational Administration, 63*–73.

Johnson, D., & Johnson, B. (2002). *High stakes.* New York, NY: Rowman & Littlefield.

Johnson, D. D., Johnson, B., Ness, D., & Farenga, S. J. (2008). *Stop high-stakes testing: An appeal to America's conscience.* Lanham, MD: Rowman & Littlefield.

Kucer, S. (2001). *Dimensions of literacy.* Mahwah, NJ: Lawrence Earlbaum.

Leithwood, K. A., Louis, K. S., Anderson, S., & Wahlstrom, K. (2004). *How leadership influences student learning: Review of research.* Minneapolis; Toronto: Center of Applied Research and Educational Improvement, University of Minnesota; Ontario Institute for Studies in Education, University of Toronto.

Marks, H. M., & Printy, S. M. (2003). Principal leadership and school performance: An integration of transformational and instructional leadership. *Educational Administration Quarterly, 39*(3), 370–397. doi: 10.1177/0013161X03253412

Matsumura, L., Sartoris, M., DiPrima Bickel, D., & Garnier, H. (2009). Leadership for literacy: The principal's role in launching a new coaching program. *Educational Administration Quarterly, 45*(5), 655–693.

McKenna, M., & Walpole, S. (2008). *The literacy coaching challenge: Models and methods for grades K-6.* New York, NY: Guilford Press.

Murray, D. M. (2003). *Writer teaches writing revised.* Boston, MA: Heinle & Heinle.

National Association of Elementary School Principals. (2001). *Standards for what principals should know and be able to do.* Alexandria, VA: National Association of Elementary School Principals.

National Policy Board for Educational Administration: Professional Standards for Educational Leaders, (2015). Reston, VA.

Neuman, S. (2009). *Changing the odds for children at risk.* New York, NY: Teachers College Press.

No Child Left Behind. (2001). *Public Law No. 107-1110, 115 Stat. 1425, 2002.* One hundred seventh Congress of the United States of America.

Prince, J., & Conaway, B. D. (1985). Principal's effect on the school reading program. *The Small School Forum, 6*(3), 1–3.

Printy, S. M., Marks, H. M., & Bowers, A. J. (2009). Integrated leadership: How principals and teachers share transformational and instructional influence. [Article]. *Journal of School Leadership, 19*(5), 504–532.

Protheroe, N. (2008). The K-8 principal in 2008: A 10-year study eighth in a series of research studies launched in 1928. Retrieved from www.naesp.org/resources/2/10_Year_Study/10-year_study-2008.pdf

Rasinski, T. (2003). *The fluent reader.* New York, NY: Scholastic.

Reeves, D. B. (2008). The leadership challenge in literacy. *Educational Leadership, 65*(7), 91–92.

Robinson, V. M. J., Lloyed, C. A., & Rowe, K. (2008). The impact of leadership on student outcomes: An analysis of the differential effects of leadership types. *Educational Administration Quarterly, 44*(5), 635–674. doi: 10.1177/0013161X08321509

Schneider, M. (2014). *A chronicle of echoes: Who's who in the implosion of American public education.* Charlotte, NC: Information Age.

Schneider, M. (2015). *Common core dilemma: Who owns our schools?* New York, NY: Teacher College Press.

Schneider, M. K. (2016). *School choice: The end of public education?* New York, NY: Teachers College Press.

Stein, J. K., & Nelson, B. S. (2003). Leadership content knowledge. *Educational Evaluation and Policy Analysis, 25*(4), 423–448.

Sulentic Dowell, M-M. (2008). Overcoming overwhelmed and reinventing normal: A district administrator's account of living in Hurricane Katrina's aftermath. *Journal of Education for Students Placed at Risk, 13*(2–3), 135–167.

Sulentic Dowell, M-M. (2012). Addressing the complexities of literacy and urban teaching in the United States: Strategic professional development as intervention. *Teaching Education Journal, 23*(1), 40–49.

Sulentic Dowell, M-M., Hoewing, B., & Bickmore, D. (2012). A framework for defining literacy leadership. *Journal of Reading Education, 37*(2), 7–15.

Tooms, A. (2003, September). Letters to Angel. *Educational Leadership, 61*(1), 82–85.

Williamson, M. (2011). Morning prayer. *The Heart of a Sacred Activist.* Retrieved from http://heartofsacredactivist.blogspot.com/2011/06/morning-prayer-by-marianne-williamson.html

Zepeda, S. J. (2007). *The principal as instructional leader: A handbook for supervisors.* Larchmont, NY: Eye on Education.

Chapter Two

Belief Statements

Belief can be a challenging construct. We all have beliefs, but have you ever considered how yours were formed? Beliefs are grounded in our personal, professional, and shared experiences. They are formed by what our families believed and passed on to us, what any caregivers or important role models in our lives impressed upon us, and what our friends and colleagues value and perhaps devalue. Our beliefs are shaped by what we have learned, what we have witnessed, and what we have experienced. Beliefs are connected to what we perceive as personal truths.

In a familial structure, shared kinship and communal experience often lead to common beliefs. Collective ways of knowing, mutual expectations, and group traditions create bonds. Shared beliefs can strengthen bonds, forge allegiances, and create a sense of fidelity among and to a group of people. Beliefs are important, and having them woven into a school's culture, like a family's culture, is paramount for the continued success of the campus as a unit. Schools are not the same as a family unit. A school's mission can function as a means to establish and promote an esprit de corps among all faculty.

Given the increased political mandates and resultant pressures and expectations surrounding all students' acquisition of adequate literacy skills, the authors draw upon research literature from the educational leadership field, suggesting the primary role of the principal is to lead instructional development, assuming the mantle of instructional leadership (Booth & Rowsell, 2007). This expectation includes providing continued support of a school's mission, a clear and compelling statement that is emblematic of the beliefs that propel the school community forward.

Hallinger and Heck (2002) recommend clearly defining the purpose or mission of the school organization and how that purpose or mission will result in a mutually desired future or vision. The explicit, attainable, and intentional outcomes or goals that support the school's mission and vision are foundational elements of a school's success. Having a clear mission sets expectations and drives decision-making.

In regard to literacy leadership, developing a literacy mission and vision while building faculty relationships and shared beliefs about literacy learning and teaching is how a principal promotes high-quality literacy instruction. This in itself is a daunting task. Layered with a multitude of managerial tasks, such as coordinating transportation and organizing services for children ranging from speech to physical therapy and everything in between, as well as managing community relationships, the role of an elementary principal as a literacy leader is complex and multifaceted. In short, principals cannot accomplish myriad responsibilities alone. Literacy leaders must work in tandem with teachers.

Principals can assist in the development of teachers by building individuals' capacity within the beliefs, mission, and vision of the organization through direct support and by facilitating access to models of effective teaching practices. Principals enhance school and student performance by building collaborative processes. Leithwood, Louis, Anderson, and Wahlstrom (2004) suggest that a principal's concerns and the time focused around supervision and management practices can result in enhanced student outcomes.

Shared instructional leadership as described by Hallinger (2003) and Hallinger and Murphy (1985) highlights that the principal sets the example for development and support of a school mission and vision, takes responsibility for managing instruction, and is the central figure in developing school culture. However, the principal cannot be the *sole* driving force in enacting mission and vision. It is also incumbent on teachers to both co-craft and accomplish the school's mission collaboratively. In a true collaborative instructional model of leadership, if the mission and vision reflect teachers' shared beliefs about teaching and learning, then teachers also shoulder responsibility in endorsing and achieving mission and vision. The following vignette is a cautionary tale that illustrates the theory of Hallinger's (2003) and Hallinger and Murphy's (1985) shared instructional leadership and the notion of Hallinger and Heck's (2002) suggested practice of collaborative mission and vision.

When Jason became principal in 2010, his school did not have any discernible shared belief statements. He believed that through his words and actions (supervision and management practices), the staff would understand what he believed in and they would naturally follow and accept his beliefs. He repeatedly reinforced to his staff his belief that teaching should be joyful, that relationships were at the core of good teaching, and that instructional auton-

omy was fundamental to student achievement as well as a professional re-spect for teachers.

Many of the teachers agreed with these beliefs, particularly veteran teachers. As veteran teacher, Millie reported,

> *I feel re-energized that I have the ability to teach based on what my kids need. I don't need to be on a certain page every day. I can go faster and slower based on what I observe. I've been teaching long enough that I know the standards and make sure I hit them by creating my own lessons. I don't need to be restricted by a resource.*

Jason was euphoric and remembers thinking, "This was liberating! Teachers were excited to have autonomy."

Jason also recalls that some teachers indicated that they were feeling like professionals, and they recognized that they were trusted to make the best instructional decisions based on the needs of their students. Jason was em-boldened. He recollects thinking that it was quite simple—you give teachers autonomy and great things will happen—but he failed to address the differ-ences between veteran and novice teachers' expertise, experience, knowl-edge base, and perhaps most importantly, their self-confidence with making instructional decisions in isolation. Jason's euphoria evaporated, and his sense of accomplishment came crashing down.

For instance, Grace, a third grade teacher with five years of teaching experience, shared a different, tearful experience with autonomy.

> *I really like that you give us choice in how to teach. I like being creative, but there is so much out there. I find myself researching and reading all the time. I never know what to pick and what to use. One person says this is the best way, and then someone else says this is the best way. It is overwhelming and exhausting. Sometimes I wish you would just tell us how to teach so it wouldn't be so exhausting.*

Grace also shared that it wasn't just the exhaustion that bothered her but also the fear.

She expressed that, left to her own decisions, she may make the wrong decision and fail her students. Hearing this, Jason was no longer embold-ened, but devastated. Had his beliefs resulted in a demoralized teacher? Had he led the faculty in his building down the wrong path?

After much reflection and soul searching, Jason decided it was not the beliefs that were wrong, but that they were his beliefs, not shared beliefs. He had neglected to discuss and share them in any way with teachers, yet erro-neously expected teachers to embrace them as their own. Jason needed to find a way for his instructional staff to develop their own beliefs collabora-

tively rather than to simply adopt his. Thus began a journey for Jason as he took steps to become a literacy leader.

WORKING TOWARD SHARED BELIEFS: GETTING THERE

The journey to shared reading beliefs began in the summer of 2012 with data day. This was a meeting between building-level and district-level administrators. Jason and his associate principal (AP), Scott, had completed a review of the school's state performance report, and as Jason recalls, "It left us feeling sick. I wanted to throw up." He reflected on the talented group of newer teachers who were being mentored by veteran teachers. However, state school report scores told a story that didn't adequately mirror what he was observing on campus and in classrooms.

Even more personally for Jason, this was the school all his children attended, and they did well. At first he was bewildered. Then he began to ask himself the following questions:

- Am I the right person for the job?
- What is really going on in classrooms?
- Are teachers doing their jobs?
- Who can help us set the vision?
- Are we on the right course?
- Why are our scores starting to fall?

Jason was grappling with the reality of the school report card, and the changing demographics of the student body. He also viewed the teachers in the building from a positive perspective because he knew they were great, committed, and hard working. He was feeling what most principals feel when the school report card or state assessment arrives: If the scores are good, there is a collective sigh of relief. If the scores are less than desired, it feels as though someone sucked all the life out of you.

Summer was a tense time. That's when the school's grades were posted for everyone to see. In the state of Wisconsin, as in states across the United States, the report card is available for public consumption, as it is a downloadable PDF on the Wisconsin Department of Public Instruction's website. Jason knew if his scores didn't improve, this school, his school, would be the most underperforming school in the district, and his leadership, the teachers' talents, and his students would be carefully scrutinized.

Jason knew that scores alone didn't sufficiently define the wide range of talents and abilities of his teachers, instructional support staff, students, or school community. After days of poring over student achievement and historical trends, the two administrators agreed that the main issue was with a particular grade level. It wasn't that the teachers at that grade level were less effective than others.

Both Jason and Scott, the school's AP, believed the targeted grade level needed support because within the team were inexperienced teachers who had, with the exception of the team leader, just recently joined the school. The solution to improved student performance was going to be answered with a comprehensive mentoring and coaching plan for the team. Jason, Scott, the director of curriculum, and the director of teaching and assessment were ecstatic, certain they had a viable solution to raising test scores.

Convinced that this was a plan of genius that the teachers would love, and a plan that would serve as a model for all other grade-level teams, Jason regained his excitement. He and Scott, along with the director of curriculum and the director of teaching and assessment in the district, could not wait to share the plan with the team. Needless to say, the plan was not met with the same level of enthusiasm by the teachers. In fact, they were deeply offended by the plan. Their response was not the result of an unwillingness to examine student performance. They were equally if not more concerned about how their students performed. They recognized the plan was developed with good intent; however, they felt like they were being targeted and labeled as poor-performing teachers.

One teacher noted, "I have my masters in reading. I serve as a mentor to new teachers, and I'm a team leader. This plan makes me feel like you believe I can't teach my kids." Another teacher summed it up by saying, "I understand the plan, but just targeting our grade level makes me pissed." These comments weighed heavily on Jason and the AP. Again, Jason's excitement waned. He experienced self-doubt, and as an elementary principal, the instructional leader, and school manager, he felt deflated and defeated.

But Jason also recognized the folly of his ways. The teachers were excluded from creating the plan and providing input. They had their own ideas. Jason reflected:

> We had called into question their professional judgment and abilities. Through continued discourse, we learned of their passion for teaching literacy. We also learned of their frustration with how they were being required to teach literacy. They had ideas that were grounded in reading research and recommended practice—framework they believed in as teachers.

The team of teachers wanted Jason and the other administrators to examine the framework and make this a schoolwide effort rather than what felt like a grade-level attack.

So that's what Jason, district-level administrators, and this group of teachers did.

The journey to a school-wide literacy initiative began with the formation of a Literacy Leadership Team at his school. This team was comprised of classroom teachers, special education teachers, Title I teachers, and building-level and district-level administrators. Teachers were selected and invited to be part of the team if they had completed advanced coursework in literacy or reading instruction. The team continued to examine student data and isolate the causes for low student performance.

After several months of meetings, the Literacy Leadership Team focused on their own professional development. The team met twice a month from 7:45 to 8:20 a.m. prior to the start of the instructional day. While there was no specific agenda, Jason and the team decided to do a book study of *Read, Write, Lead* by Regie Routman (2014). The only expectation was that the team members would read the assigned chapters and be ready to share their impressions. It was Jason's role to facilitate the discussion without dominating. Striking this balance was challenging. As the principal, he felt a need to have a strong voice to validate *his* position.

With the assistance of supportive team members, they provided him feedback when they thought he was monopolizing the conversation. After each discussion the team set a goal: identify one specific literacy growth area or one approach they would share with a grade-level team. Much of the direction came from team members as a grassroots approach to making literacy a more intentional focus of the school.

In the summer of 2012, the fifteen members of the Literacy Leadership Team attended a daylong conference in Madison, Wisconsin, at which Regie Routman was the featured speaker. The conference allowed for team planning guided by Regie Routman. At the end of the day, the members of the Literacy Leadership Team agreed that they needed a more specific plan for literacy instruction at their school, and they wanted it to involve *all teachers*. They also agreed that while they believed in much of Regie Routman's philosophy, they did not want to become Routman disciples. Instead, they wanted to create a literacy-rich environment that reflected the unique needs of their students and the teachers at their elementary school.

MAKING THE BELIEFS COME ALIVE

The clarity for Jason was that his building was void of a set of shared beliefs. He thought he was making beliefs clear through words and actions. Jason had never concretely identified the beliefs that he wanted the building to ascribe to, live out through practice, and align their teaching to in a clear and concise way. He never articulated the importance of teaching literacy nor acknowledged the reality that some teachers didn't like to teach literacy. In fact,

Jason found that the teachers who didn't like to teach reading were actually some of his best reading teachers.

The lack of articulated beliefs impacted the school culture, but Jason was determined to reset the path to ensure his teachers experienced joy and autonomy. In his building of over one hundred staff members, they worked hard to create a set of shared reading beliefs. This was not an easy feat. Their process included:

- Reflecting on one's relationship with reading personally
- Reflecting on one's relationship with reading professionally

Similar to a reading interest inventory, teachers were asked to respond to the following prompts:

- What do I like to read?
- Who do I like to read?
- When do I like to read?
- What do I dislike most about reading?
- What do I like most about reading?

Modeling this process and engaging in this level of reflection was new to many teachers. Teachers were not accustomed to be asked to be vulnerable as learners in this way. This reflective process was also a new way for Jason to get to know his teachers and to think differently about professional development, particularly considering the makeup of the building, which, three years prior, was composed primarily of teachers with ten or more years of experience and now was composed primarily of teachers with five or fewer years of experience.

The instructional staff agreed that these beliefs would serve as the guide for instructional decision-making. Any decisions made regarding curriculum, instructional resources, scheduling, or other items were determined by how they fit within the framework of collaboratively held reading beliefs. Because all were involved in the process, everyone shared ownership in the beliefs. They were the fabric of the school culture and emblematic of the school's literacy mission and vision. Figure 2.1 shows a poster displaying these collaboratively held reading beliefs.

BREATHING LIFE INTO LITERACY BELIEFS

It is one thing to have universal agreement for reading beliefs, but displaying posters of the beliefs in every classroom does not guarantee a cultural shift. And discussing beliefs can only move faculty forward so far. Breathing life

Student choice and easy access to books influence motivation and achievement.

Time should be made for read alouds and independent reading on a regular basis.

Positive relationships and connections can be built through reading.

Figure 2.1. Westwood Elementary School Reading Beliefs

into beliefs and making them part of the school's cultural fabric required intentionality and planning. Intentionality became the focus of the Literacy Leadership Team. The following steps illustrate the process of creating and enacting a literacy vision and mission through the creation of collaborative reading beliefs that Jason shared with his teachers.

Faculty Meetings

Jason and his instructional staff made the reading beliefs part of the monthly faculty meetings. The first step was helping teachers to understand what the reading beliefs looked like instructionally. Faculty meetings were intention-ally designed to describe to teachers what student choice looked like in the classroom. It is one thing to allow elementary-aged children to self-select books. It is another to allow so much choice that teachers had little or no input into what students were reading. The faculty finally settled on free choice coupled with directed choice. Students and teachers came to understand that choice was not unlimited.

This was not easy. While everyone had agreed on student choice as one of the belief statements, agreeing on how that looked in classrooms was an unanticipated challenge. Perhaps the greatest struggle was at library checkout. It was a difficult transition to allow students to check out books of their choice even when the books were well beyond their reading ability. However, the belief in student choice did not change. If students wanted a certain book, they were allowed to access it because they showed interest and a desire to read the material.

Such issues as these were intentionally discussed at faculty meetings. Teachers had to wrestle with how choice was to be managed and facilitated. Time was devoted for teachers to brainstorm how to encourage student choice and how to assist students in picking books. Prior to the adoption of student choice as a belief, student book selection was mainly guided by the teacher. Students had to learn how to choose appropriate books, and teachers needed professional development assistance on how to make this happen. Members of the Literacy Leadership Team were instrumental in assisting with this process.

Beyond the reading belief grounded in student choice, teachers had to restructure their schedules to accommodate for independent reading time and time for read-alouds. This was difficult. While many teachers expressed that read-alouds were some of their most joyful times of the day, they also felt it was stressful. The stress was a result of the demands placed on the teachers to get through the curriculum.

The demands were not direct edicts from Jason or district-level administrators. In fact, the message from administration was to be responsive to students and take the time necessary to adequately present new information. However, the teachers had a hard time internalizing this feeling because of their concern they were not doing the best they could for their students or not moving fast enough through the curriculum.

As one teacher noted, "I know we are supposed to slow down and spend time with read-alouds, but when the discussion goes long, I begin to lose my focus. I worry about the time and what I'm not getting done rather than being present in the moment and capturing that learning." This sentiment emphasized the importance of listening to teachers and helping them to find ways to celebrate their success and their students' success as well as how to manage the stress associated with getting it all done.

During faculty meetings, time was devoted to professional development activities in which teachers were encouraged to make read-aloud and independent reading time a priority in their schedule. The teachers were grounded in knowing that to make students better readers, students needed to spend more time reading and having fluent reading modeled. This may seem trite, but they needed both permission and support to spend time reading aloud and having students read independently without feeling they were doing something that was not connected to the standards being assessed.

Finally, faculty meetings also focused on developing strategies for using children's literature to build relationships with students. Perhaps the most surprising moment was realizing that not all teachers are proficient or natural in forming relationships with students. To address this, all teachers were asked to complete a reading history map. The map illustrated how they had developed relationships with reading from their childhood to their current age. The map was a visual representation of each teacher's journey as a reader.

The staff shared their reading maps in small groups and then in the larger group. The transparency and honesty shared among the teachers created a shared experience. They learned that some of their colleagues did not enjoy reading as a child, and some even didn't like to read as adults. Teachers were able to articulate why or share turning points where they were not interested in reading and then became lovers of reading. Others shared their interests in reading beyond texts and discussed how they preferred digital reading or podcasts.

The teaching staff left these discussions and shared experiences with a deep understanding of their colleagues' views on reading. The collective self-awareness was transformational, and what the teachers experienced translated to a better understanding of one another. Most importantly, these shared experiences also translated their understanding of students who either liked or did not like to read.

Celebrating Success

The reading beliefs were made a permanent fixture of the school's literacy vision and instructional culture. Celebrating the beliefs became an important part of faculty meetings. To begin a faculty meeting, Jason would recognize teachers who had demonstrated implementation of the reading beliefs as a result of his observations. While this sounds insignificant, and possibly childish, it became an important tradition, emblematic of faculty beliefs.

Jason awarded superhero figurines to teachers who had demonstrated the reading beliefs within their classroom. If he had observed a teacher allowing students to choose a book that was of high interest to them, but not at their level (either above or below), he would note that and share it at the faculty meeting. If he observed a read-aloud, he would acknowledge a teacher for the level of engagement displayed by the students, the teacher-questioning techniques, or the use of different voices during the read-aloud.

Finally, he would recognize teachers who had built a relationship with students by recommending books to their students that matched their interests. Eventually, he opened the floor and allowed teachers to award superhero figurines to each other for implementation of the reading beliefs. Jason and his teachers looked forward to superhero faculty meetings. Everyone left feeling good and valued for what they had accomplished.

FINAL THOUGHTS ON SHARED READING BELIEFS

This may all seem like common sense, but it is deeper than that. Jason believed that his personal literacy vision was enough to move his teachers and his students forward. But he learned a powerful lesson, grounded in the research from the educational leadership field: he needed to involve teachers in key decisions such as creating literacy belief statements.

Jason was reminded of the efficacy of Hallinger and Heck's (2002) recommendations. Jason focused his efforts on clearly defining the purpose or mission of the school and how that purpose or mission would result in a mutually desired outcome. In terms if literacy leadership, the vision of the principal is critical in the success of the school. However, a shared set of beliefs and a shared vision developed by all, not a small committee or one individual, is so much more powerful than any one person's vision or set of beliefs.

When the faculty agreed to a shared set of reading beliefs, they made a commitment to their students and to each other. They agreed to make the elements of choice, time, and relationships part of a strong fabric of the school culture. They also agreed to say, "This is who we are," and to hold each other accountable to living the beliefs. In many ways, this exercise brought joy back into the teaching lives of the faculty under Jason's supervision. And with that joy came a renewed sense of professionalism and self-efficacy.

The long-term effects on student achievement are not known at the time of this publication. The short-term data from statewide assessments show a positive trend upward in reading scores. Perhaps most important were the anecdotal notes and messages that Jason has received from parents expressing that their children are more interested in and motivated to spend time reading. And teachers had a shared belief in core literacy practices, something that bound them together and carried them through the intense, complex work of teaching.

In regard to literacy leadership, developing a literacy mission and vision is imperative. This aspect of the mission creates a sense of clarity around what literacy means and looks like for teachers and students alike. A literacy mission and vision operates in tandem with building faculty relationships and shared beliefs about literacy learning. Most of all, this is one way that a principal can encourage and promote high-quality literacy instruction.

WHERE DO BELIEFS EXIST?

Most schools may have similar-sounding belief statements. The statements are grounded in helping students become productive citizens and lifelong-learners, in promoting diversity, in integrating technology, and in helping students feel respected, valued, and safe. It is hard to imagine many people who would not consider belief statements grounded in the aforementioned list to be anything other than worthy.

Belief statements that become part of the cultural fabric of a school organization are transformative. Belief statements are the foundation for transformation because they become deeply rooted in the culture of the building. Teachers begin to make curricular and instructional decisions based on the reading beliefs of choice, time, and relationships. If the instructional practice does not match the reading beliefs, then it is not practiced. When a school gets to that level of transformation, it becomes intentionally focused on how students experience learning and what is learned.

Construction of belief statements can be a messy process. This chapter highlights the challenges when beliefs are not articulated clearly but also the benefits of engaging a collaborative process to create a culture where beliefs are known and agreed on. In writing this chapter, the authors recognize that beliefs articulated by the literacy leader must also align with the overall mission of the district. Building specific beliefs as described in the chapter are meant to inform culture and set the foundation for decision-making. Chapter 3 transitions from beliefs to joy. Joy in the next chapter is a result of having beliefs and seeing them enacted as instruction.

REFLECTION QUESTIONS

- Search for your school or school district's belief statements; what did you find?
- Who created these belief statements?
- If belief statements do not exist, or if it is time for revision, who needs to be engaged in this process?
- As a literacy leader, what would it look like in your building if these beliefs were part of the fabric of teaching and learning?

REFERENCES

Booth, D., & Rowsell, J. (2007). *The literacy principal, leading, supporting, and assessing reading and writing initiatives* (2nd ed.). Portland, ME: Stenhouse.

Hallinger, P. (2003). Leading educational change: Reflections on the practice of instructional and transformational leadership. *Cambridge Journal of Education, 33*(3), 329–351. doi: 10.1080/0305764032000122005

Hallinger, P., & Heck, R. H. (2002). What do we call people with vision? The role of vision, mission and goals in school leadership and improvement. In K. A. Leithwood (Ed.), *Second international handbook of educational leadership and administration* (pp. 9–40). Dordrecht; Boston, MA: Kluwer.

Hallinger, P., & Murphy, J. (1985). Assessing the instructional management behavior of principals. *Elementary School Journal, 86*(2), 217–247.

Leithwood, K. A., Louis, K. S., Anderson, S., & Wahlstrom, K. (2004). *How leadership influences student learning: Review of research.* Toronto, Canada: Center of Applied Research and Educational Improvement; Ontario Institute for Studies in Education, University of Toronto.

Routeman, R. (2014). *Read, write, lead: Breakthrough strategies for school-wide literacy success.* Alexandria, VA: Association for Supervision and Curriculum Development.

Chapter Three

The Principal's Role in Creating a Culture of Joy

Joy (noun): the emotion evoked by well-being, success, or good fortune or by the prospect of possessing what one desires.—Merriam-Webster.com

WHAT IS JOY?

Joy is happiness. Joy is satisfaction. Joy is contentment. Joy is fulfillment. Joy is measurable. As a reader, you may question why we're writing about joy. In his 2008 article for *Educational Leadership* magazine, Steven Wolk specifically addresses joy within the context of educational environments. For Wolk (2008), joy in school is represented by these ten important concepts.

1. Finding pleasure in learning
2. Giving students choice
3. Allowing students to create
4. Showing off student work
5. Letting students tinker
6. Making school spaces inviting
7. Getting outside
8. Reading good books
9. Offering more physical education and art classes
10. Transforming assessment

Most educators reading the aforementioned list may agree with each of the ten concepts but may be challenged to adopt any one of them because of the demands of the following:

- time;
- political mandates;
- directives from district/central office; and
- potentially unsupportive administrators.

Unfortunately, when these challenges converge, it creates a perfect storm that eliminates joy from the classroom, school, and entire district.

As school leaders read this list, they may think, "This is all feel-good, touchy-feely stuff, but this won't improve student achievement or test scores. Besides, even if we *did* want to focus on joy, there simply isn't any time." Principals in elementary schools, where one would assume teachers and students have the most joy, will hear teachers lament, "This is great, but show me where and when I get the time to do any of this."

In fact, elementary school principals must attempt to create the conditions where joy is enmeshed into the fabric of the school culture. Unfortunately, for school leaders, thinking and talking about joy may seem ridiculous in this day and age. However, the authors argue that by increasing the number of joyful experiences within a school, teachers will find joy in coming to work and will engage students in creative lessons, and test scores may, in fact, increase.

These ten important concepts, when acted on with intentionality, will shift the culture among teachers and change how students and staff experience school. This list can inform how elementary principals lead, provide feedback to teachers, and create a culture where joy is tangible.

FINDING PLEASURE IN LEARNING

Learning as a pleasurable experience is not synonymous with being a "lifelong learner." Most educators will say, "I am a lifelong learner." As humans we are always learning, but what does it mean to *take pleasure in learning*? For a school administrator or teacher leader, finding pleasure in learning can be difficult. With an increased number of mandated assessments and pressure to demonstrate acceptable test scores, a focus on the joy and wonder within learning is often left by the wayside.

School leaders and educators don't have to leave the pleasure of learning behind. It is the role of the school principal and his or her teacher leaders to create the conditions to empower teachers and their students to rediscover the joy of learning. The school principal can create the conditions to provide space for teachers and students to learn that is within the prescribed standards and also evoke a sense of wonder in students. When we create the conditions for teachers to find joy in their own learning, they transfer the joy of learning to their students.

GIVING STUDENTS CHOICE

Students do not experience choice often, particularly when it comes to their learning. Additionally, many school leaders limit teacher choice. In many public school systems, choice is not in anyone's vocabulary. To foster a culture of choice means fostering a culture that supports and encourages teachers to be decision-makers.

We learn things based on our individual passions and interests. However, so much of the current educational system does not value choice within the classroom. The current system supports developing compliant students who can perform well on standardized tests, void of joy.

Cultivating joy in your school may be challenging. As an administrator, you must be willing to grant teachers the freedom to make choices. Administrators must repeatedly remind teachers that they have the power to make professional decisions about what their students need to learn. No prescribed instructional program can grant that level of choice. It is up to the teachers to make those decisions, not the curricular program manual.

Consider this example as a way to facilitate teacher and student choice: Jason has a veteran primary grade teacher who is highly skilled in her delivery of content and traditional in her approach to classroom design and student management. Her classroom is designed with rows of desks with all students facing the front of the classroom. This teacher enjoys the "sage on the stage" approach to instruction. There is a kidney-shaped table for small group instruction, a classroom library, and a place for students to gather in front of the teacher's rocking chair. Students are expected to be quiet listeners and follow the directives of the teacher.

On a walk-through, Jason witnessed the teacher giving her students the choice and control to redesign their seating arrangement. At first glance, this may not seem to be a major change in the instructional approach. What may look like a minor change was in fact a *major* paradigm shift for the teacher. Here's how she did it.

The veteran teacher gave her students a few parameters. She needed certain spaces open for whole-group instruction, and she needed to make sure all of the students could see her from where they placed their desks when she was instructing. With those instructions, she let her students redesign their seating arrangement. As the teacher stood off to the side, she allowed the

Chapter 3

students to debate, explore, make changes, and settle disagreements about desk placement without her interference.

Watching the students was fascinating. Watching the teacher was remarkable. The anxiety and tension radiating from her could be felt from across the room. She was doing something that was difficult for her. However, in spite of how difficult it was for her, she remained grounded in giving her students choice.

She gave up control in order to give more control to her students. After the process was done, she wondered why she had waited so long to feel comfortable to allow her students more choice. Upon reflection, she stated it was because she felt she had never been given the permission to explore choice in the classroom. Now that she knew her administrators supported teacher and student choice, she felt liberated. Because of her willingness to push herself, Jason celebrated her efforts at the next faculty meeting with an instructional superhero award.

Without offering choice, we run the risk of students becoming disengaged and disenfranchised learners. A word of caution: the authors are not advocating that students get to choose not to learn math. They have to learn math to be successful outside of school. Students may not choose what *content* they want to learn; how they learn it and how they demonstrate their learning should include choice.

ALLOWING STUDENTS TO CREATE

Creation is the highest level of Bloom's Taxonomy (Anderson et al., 2001). Creation requires time, mistakes, and revisions. The process of creating something is often inspiring and can be life-giving. Most likely you have experienced euphoric feelings of joy when you've created something. The same feelings you experience when you create, students also experience when they have the opportunity to create. A closer look at the thought processes that are involved in creation will find that it is rich with lifelong lessons of problem-solving, perseverance, satisfaction, and work ethic. Who can argue those are skills we would not want our staff, colleagues, and students to have?

SHOWING OFF STUDENT WORK

Don't hide your students' light under a bushel basket. Student work should be displayed where it can be seen and celebrated. Oftentimes the student work is not effectively displayed to highlight student learning, student decision-making, or creative abilities. Student work is often placed in hallways, but near the top of the ceiling.

Imagine a five-year-old trying to crane his neck to see his writing or drawing that is eight feet off the floor. The reality is he can't, and therefore, in his world, his work is never displayed. You might be able to guess why the work was displayed so high—so the students couldn't touch it. How ridiculous. Not only could they not touch the work, but they could also not see it. In fact, many adults even had a hard time reading it.

In an effort to apply this concept in your building, work with facilities to lower the tack strips so student work is at students' eye level. And there is more you can do to ensure student work is displayed, celebrated, and commented on in its authentic form. Think how powerful it might be for students to read comments from other students, parents, teachers, or administrators about their work. Think of how joyful and proud the students will be when they share those things with their loved ones at home.

LETTING STUDENTS TINKER

Similar to allowing students to create, tinkering is an important strategy that can create joy in the classroom. Tinkering is taking things you know don't work—old phones, computers, TVs, clocks, and so on—and allowing students the opportunity to take them apart and put them back together. It is not always about making everything new and completely functional, but there should be space for recreation and repurposing or mere exploration.

Tinkering allows the students to explore the inner complexity of items and determine how they work. It is rare that students will actually fix an item, but the interest that is piqued by exploring creates a sense of joy in the process of learning.

MAKING SCHOOL SPACES INVITING

What if an early career teacher asks to redesign his classroom by eliminating desks? Jason was presented with this exact scenario. During a reflective conversation, a first-year teacher shared that during his student teaching experience in New Zealand, his cooperating teacher used flexible seating, and he felt that the flexible seating aided in creating an environment in which students were more comfortable and engaged.

As a principal, your initial reaction might be filled with trepidation. Many questions might swirl in your mind:

- How could we eliminate desks?
- What would parents think?
- What would the superintendent and school board think?

However, one word should keep entering your mind: *choice*. The teacher had done his research. He made a compelling argument that student learning is at the core of his decision to make the changes.

Finally, you might grant this teacher permission to make the changes with the conditions that if a student wanted a desk, a student would be given one. If the teacher was unable to manage the classroom and the new seating arrangement, then all the desks would be returned to the classroom. As a leader, you are still grappling between what has been done and what might be great for kids.

Jason let the teacher try it, take the risk, and be a professional. The changes to the classroom benefited the students in many ways. It facilitated a stronger classroom community by creating the expectations for how to appropriately use the furniture. Students came to realize what types of learning spaces work best for them and how to make personal decisions when their learning was not benefiting from their choices. Other teachers saw the positive impacts and began exploring the idea of flexible seating for their own classrooms. Finally, the authors found students would rather learn in a classroom that included no desks, but rather a rowboat filled with pillows, beanbag chairs, a cocoon swing, and multiple types of seating arrangements.

GETTING OUTSIDE

In many schools, the opportunity for students to get outside and enjoy recess has been eliminated in an effort to increase time for instruction. Across the country, recess has been replaced with brain breaks that are five to ten minutes long and involve kids following dance routines on the classroom Smart Board.

While the brain break serves a purpose, it cannot replace the joy that is experienced when children are allowed to design their own games and engage in imaginative play outside during recess. Too much time is spent managing our students' time. Instead, let them go and explore the wonders of the grass, rocks, birds, and bugs. Children are naturally inquisitive; they will learn because they are following their interests in a joyful pursuit of knowledge.

READING GOOD BOOKS

In a blog post by Pernille Ripp (2017), she highlights the need for students to read good books. In her English class of middle school students, she found that the majority of students reported they disliked—and in some cases hated—reading. She remedied this by allowing her students to read books of their choice and from multiple genres. At the end of the year, only 14 percent of her students reported they still disliked reading, but not as much as they did at the beginning of the year.

If we think deeper about this, it highlights the importance of building a love of reading in elementary school. A great deal of time at the elementary level is spent teaching the *skills* of reading, but little time is devoted to teaching the love of reading. Both can exist in the same classroom, but only when we recognize that done correctly, reading good books is a joyful and a life-changing event.

Struggling readers want to read good books. However, they will not have that opportunity if the focus is on providing books that focus on skill development and not joy development. Although many elementary school principals are not trained as literacy specialists, they recognize the need for on-level and instructional-level texts, but there are also times and spaces for struggling readers to choose a book that seems interesting.

ADDING MORE PHYSICAL EDUCATION AND ART CLASSES

In the era of diminishing school budgets, physical education, art, and music classes can be some of the first areas eliminated from the schedule. This is a travesty! Students who are more physically active perform better in school and are more self-regulated, happy people. Likewise, the joy in expressing themselves through art and music unlocks the often-neglected intelligence held in the fine arts. Robinson and Aronica (2015) often speak of the ways our schools are removing creativity from the lives of our children. To create a joyful environment, our kids must have the freedom to express their gifts in other ways than academic achievement measures.

TRANSFORMING ASSESSMENT

The authors of this book are not against assessment. In fact, assessment is critical to understanding the learning needs of our students. What they are against is the enormity and complexity of the assessments teachers are required to administer. Testing has gotten in the way of student learning.

Most students want feedback on their progress. Feedback can be fulfilling and a springboard for future growth. However, when assessments are standardized and universal, they fail to recognize the varying ways students demonstrate learning. This assessment-heavy culture has inadvertently removed the joy from the learning process.

Students' achievement should not be based on their ability to understand how to take a test. Assessments should be transformed so they can adequately assess student progress in a way that allows the students to demonstrate proficiency of their learning without fear of the test structure getting in the way. Literacy leaders should commit to creating joyful learning experiences. In addition, they should consider and align assessment practices to be just as joyful for students. When students are part of the assessment process, it becomes a student-owned endeavor. As a result, students and teachers find the process of assessment to be more enjoyable and productive (Carr & Bryson, 2017).

While the ten concepts presented earlier in this chapter seem simple and easy, there are many challenges to incorporating all ten in any elementary school and classroom. The authors recognize the political landscape where compliance and accountability are primary on the agenda. Creating an educational environment for early learners where joy is experienced daily probably never appears as an agenda item for staff meetings, district-level principal meetings, or school board meetings.

Individuals in the aforementioned roles are not interested in joy in the classroom. Any efforts to speak of joy or the values of joy are met with a scoff. If teachers speak of joy, they are labeled as teachers who are lazy and don't want to be held accountable to the standards of student learning. In fact, it will be their commitment to finding joyful experiences in the classroom that is targeted as the cause of a failing school system.

Negative reactions to joy are puzzling. Maybe not puzzling—but maddening. Maybe even infuriating. The negative reactions to joy and a demand for teacher and student compliance are counterintuitive to motivational research. "While complying can be an effective strategy for physical survival, it's a lousy one for personal fulfillment. Living a satisfying life requires more than simply meeting the demands of those in control. Yet in our offices and our classrooms we have way too much compliance and way too little engagement. The former might get you through the day, but only the latter will get you through the night" (Pink, 2009, p. 110). Making joyful practices a priority will create a paradigm shift from compliance to engagement and empowerment.

CREATING A CULTURE OF JOY: WHAT GETS IN THE WAY?

Creating a school culture where joy is valued is hard but not impossible work. Many elementary school principals will hear teachers say, "This is great, but show me where and when I get the time to do any of this." In some cases, teachers have worked to change how they conduct business in their classroom, and when they have, they have experienced feelings of increased joy, and they notice their students being more joyful throughout the day.

Consider how one teacher made a change in the way he was building math fact fluency with his students and the impact it had on his joy and that of his students. About midyear the teacher was finding his students were struggling to learn their basic math facts. After trying all of the standard math fact practices with limited success, he reflected on his practice. You can imagine what some of the intervention strategies were:

- math fact drills;
- one-minute quizzes; and
- math fact homework sheets.

After much reflection and review of his students' data, he used his professional intuition and the freedom of instructional choice to change his practice. He had realized the standard math fact practice was not connecting with the students. They were struggling to see the purpose, and it had become something to avoid rather than enjoy.

On the next day when students began their transition to math fact practice, he stopped his class and let them know they would be learning a game instead of doing the daily math fact drills. He gave them each a cribbage board and taught them to play cribbage. He shared with them how much cribbage meant to him. The vulnerability of this teacher allowed him to connect with his students in a humanistic way and fostered a deeper relationship with students as learners. The authors discuss the value of teacher vulnerability and relationships later in this text.

The teacher shared his memories of playing cribbage with his grandpa and how it helped him improve his mental math. The students were hooked. After two weeks, the student data had improved. The teacher and students were ecstatic. Most importantly, the students could not wait to play cribbage and other math-related board games as a way to improve their math facts. For the teacher, the greatest moment was when one of his students shared with him that over the weekend he had spent time playing cribbage with his grandfather. It's amazing what a little joy can do.

While trying to create a culture in which teachers are more joyful, exhaustion is the unfortunate consequence. Teachers will become more tired when nothing is ever taken off their already-overflowing plate. As soon as they see the benefit from their changes, they must stop because it is time for one of the mandated district or state assessments. This is disheartening to the teacher and to the students. It is hard to be joyful in the face of continued joyless assessments.

The joy of learning is being replaced by assessments that have little authenticity to what students have been learning or the way in which they have been learning the material. The cycle becomes demoralizing and undermines the teacher as a professional. More tragically, students are demoralized by this process and lose the desire to be learners.

Most kindergarten students come through the doors of school with the enthusiasm to learn. It does not matter their ethnic background, how much money their parents make, or their race; they enter the school excited and ready to learn to read, to learn math and science and to explore the world around them.

Sadly, we've all watched those same kindergarten students, one by one, lose the joy in learning. It happens not overnight but over time. By first grade, the same students who enjoyed spending time in creative play are now struggling to maintain their attention while in reading. As the same students progressed through school, they become lethargic in their approach to learning.

By the time students enroll in a project-based school, they have become convinced that they don't like school because "it's not fun." Students might say things like "I don't get math" or "I'm not a good reader" or "I can't take tests" or that school is simply "boring." The students' negative responses about school are in direct correlation to the lack of time to create and to engage in joyful learning experiences. In addition, students are subjected to a system that values their test score more than they value them as a person.

Parents want to send their children to schools and classrooms in which the day is rich with joyful learning. Students want teachers who are joyful and passionate about teaching. Teachers want to create environments in which their students are excited about learning and find it a fulfilling and joyful experience. Herein lies the conflict. Establishing a joyful school culture in an age in which joy is not directly assessed by the mandated school accountability measures can be difficult if not impossible. To steal and modify a quote from President Kennedy, "We don't choose to make joy part of our culture because it is easy; we choose to make joy part of the culture because it is hard."

JOY AS THE FOUNDATION FOR SCHOOL CULTURE

One of the most prominent figures in the study of school culture is Dr. Kent Peterson from the University of Wisconsin–Madison. Peterson (1994) defines *school culture* as "the set of norms, values and beliefs, rituals and ceremonies, symbols and stories that make up the 'persona' of the school" (p. 10).

Culture is woven into the fabric of the belief system and operations of the school. Greunert and Whitaker (2015) suggest that school culture is created using building blocks that include:

* mission and vision
* language
* routines
* rituals

- ceremonies
- stories
- heroes
- values and beliefs (p. 28)

These are all important to establishing a strong school culture. But one thing is missing: the concept of joy within a school culture. Joy may be embedded within the building blocks, but if it is not specifically named, it runs the risk of being dismissed as a fundamental concept of strong school culture and a critical concept that students need to experience daily.

RECLAIMING JOY

Joy and joyful learning have been unintentionally removed from instructional practices and school culture because joy is viewed as an end result, not part of the foundation. Shawn Achor (2010) may help literacy leaders rethink where joy fits within school culture. Achor demonstrates that the cycle is broken. In fact, it is backward. Consider this excerpt from his book, *The Happiness Advantage*:

> If success causes happiness, then every employee who gets a promotion, every student who receives an acceptance letter, everyone who has ever accomplished a goal of any kind should be happy. But with each victory, our goalposts of success keep getting pushed further and further out, so that happiness gets pushed over the horizon.
>
> Even more important, the formula is broken because it is backward. More than a decade of groundbreaking research in the fields of positive psychology and neuroscience has proven in no uncertain terms that the relationship between success and happiness works the other way around. Thanks to this cutting-edge science, we now know that happiness is the precursor to success, not merely the result. And that happiness and optimism actually fuel performance and achievement—giving us the competitive edge that I call the Happiness Advantage. (pp. 1–2)

If the concept of joy is named and embedded as part of a school's culture, then it would follow that teacher and student success will be fueled.

THE PRINCIPAL'S ROLE IN CREATING A CULTURE OF JOY

The principal is the most important person in the school to facilitate a joyful culture. This is not opinion, but supported by research. As Habegger (2008) cites, in 2000, the Institute for Educational Leadership released findings that revealed "the single most influential factor in improving schools is the effectiveness of the principal." "Yes, all the other roles and responsibilities of a

school principal are important. But a positive school culture is imperative"
(Habegger, 2008, p. 43).

The pressure placed on the principal to assess, as well as nurture and
grow, the culture and climate of the school is enormous. Along with growing
a strong culture, the principal has the added pressure of guaranteeing the
academic progress of all students. If the principal's focus becomes singular,
the overall effectiveness of school culture and student performance suffer. To
begin to nurture and grow not only a positive school culture but also one that
has its foundation as joy, the principal must do a few things:

- be joyful;
- recognize joyful practices;
- support joyful practices; and
- cultivate a culture of joy even when it is difficult.

THE JOYFUL PRINCIPAL

Principals handle teacher observations, district-level meetings, budgets,
emails, parent phone calls, student discipline, building maintenance, transportation issues—sometimes all before 10:00 a.m. Sounds joyful, doesn't it?
All of these tasks are critical to a successfully managed school and district.
However, each has the power to eliminate the joy from the culture of a
school. If the principal becomes focused on the daily issues that prevent his
or her from doing the important work of nurturing a culture of joy, his or her
ability to create a joyful culture becomes impossible.

Principals do not become principals to create budgets, answer emails, or
focus on parent phone calls. They become principals to have a greater influence on student learning and to motivate their teachers and students to
achieve at high levels. Focusing on Shawn Achor's work, principals are
reminded that making the daily "to do" list a priority will not promote happiness or joy, and students, staff, and they, themselves, will be less productive.

It is naive to think that a principal can exude joy every moment of every
school day. However, if joy is the foundation of the school culture, then it
must be a priority. The importance of the principal's expression of joy will
permeate the building. As Whitaker (2003) states, "When the principal
sneezes, the entire building catches a cold" (p. 30). It is the authors' intent
that when the joyful principal sneezes, the entire building is filled with joy.

JOYFUL PRACTICES IN ACTION

There are times during the school year when the demands of being elementary principals can become exhausting. All of the demands on their time

become overwhelming. They can feel the joy exiting their systems. Every little thing annoys them. When they get like this, they know that kids and teachers avoid them. Teachers may even send messages asking each other, "What kind of mood is the principal in today?" When this happens, the culture within the school suffers for teachers, parents, and most importantly, students.

Principals often credit their administrative assistants, who know how to get them out of these joyless times. An administrative assistant might wander into a principal's office with a legal pad and pen and say, "You're grumpy, and frankly I'm sick of it; everyone is sick of it. Get out and visit classrooms." Like dropping the microphone at the end of a great concert, she drops the pen and legal pad on the table, making the next steps for the principal clear.

And when principals leave their offices and go visit classrooms, without fail, a magical transformation occurs. While visiting classrooms, they notice the work of the students and the teachers, which immediately reminds them of the importance of their work and the magic that happens in classrooms every day. Visiting classrooms will be the single most important thing they do to promote joy. With each visit, teachers should receive a handwritten, nonevaluative note about what the principal saw and liked, or a reflective question.

The authors recommend you try adding a hashtag to these nonevaluative notes. The hashtag at the bottom of the note sums up the visit. Below are a few hashtags the authors have left for teachers:

- #CREATINGCOMMUNITY
- #MASTERTEACHER
- #KEEPING'EMENGAGED
- #JOYFULLEARNING
- #DEEPLEARNING
- #THEYAREPOETSANDTHEYKNOWIT
- #KICKINGASS

To the authors' pleasant surprise, they discovered that leaving the notes and the hashtags provoked such joy with teachers. It actually began as a bit of a joke with one teacher. But instead of remaining a joke, other teachers commented on wanting to receive a hashtag. They kept every note and every hashtag—sometimes even comparing the hashtags with one another.

The hashtags became such an expectation that if Jason visited a classroom and didn't leave a note, he received emails or was stopped in the hall and asked why there was no note. This one gesture had become part of the culture. It was transformative. It changed how Jason scheduled his time. On his calendar, he schedules time each day to visit five to nine classrooms.

His goal is to visit each classroom every week. He averages about an 83 percent visitation rate. It's not perfect, but it's a start, and most importantly, the teachers receive recognition for their efforts and know that Jason experiences the greatest joy when he is in their classrooms. You know who else pays attention? The students. They are more than eager to share what they are working on and what they are learning. A visit from the principal is no longer a negative experience; it's a joyful experience. If you are interested in making joy a cornerstone of your school's culture, classroom visits must be a part of it.

Creating a school culture founded on joy must also include teacher autonomy in instructional practices as a core operational belief. Grounded in the work by Daniel Pink, the authors know that people are more engaged, creative, and productive when given opportunities to be autonomous in their work. For principals, it is critical to promote teacher autonomy. Too often the newest materials, programs, and technology consume principals. These things can become the drivers of principals' decisions, and they remove the human decision-making from teaching. They expect that good teachers will implement the prescribed program with fidelity, and when they do, their students will learn, and everyone will be happy. This is not reality. What really happens is that new programs come and go, and teachers learn to outlast new programs and initiatives rather than improving instructional practices.

To be clear, autonomy is not to be confused with doing whatever you want. Autonomy within the confines of the adopted standards is what the authors are advocating. Teachers should be provided with the resources they need to meet the standards, but how they use those resources is up to their professional judgment. What is happening within the field of education currently is that autonomy and professional judgment are being removed from the classroom in favor of a lockstep curricular process that ignores the individual needs of students and teachers. Sounds joyful, doesn't it?

Principals need to advocate for their teachers to have autonomy in the classroom. Allowing for autonomy will make the job of the principal more challenging because principals will need to make sure their teachers have been prepared to make well-informed instructional decisions based on the needs of their students. But the challenge is worth it. The payoff is more engaged teachers, more engaged students, and a building where teachers and students want to be because their expertise and individual needs are valued and celebrated.

Finally, if joy is important to teachers, then it is equally, if not more, important to students. While teacher autonomy is critical to creating a joyful culture, so is student autonomy. If students feel they have some control over their learning and experience a joyful classroom setting, then their learning will increase. Jason has witnessed it in his own building. After four years of focusing on joy and autonomy, the scales of academic achievement are improving. There have not been any significant changes to the instructional resources or curriculum at Jason's school. He and his staff have just focused on being joyful in their approach to instruction and autonomous in their decision-making. This has not been easy.

Being joyful and autonomous is scary and challenging. As third grade teacher Grace noted, "I sometimes wish you just told us what to do. Then we wouldn't have to make the decisions. It's hard and exhausting. I know it's the right thing, but it's exhausting." It is exhausting, but as fifth grade teacher Linda reports, she has never felt more alive in her teaching: "Now that I have autonomy, I know I can make the decisions my kids need. I don't feel the pressure to simply get through things. We get to spend time understanding content. I'm happier as a teacher. That has to be good for my students." If Linda's students recognize she is a happier teacher, then they may actually be happier students.

Recent findings regarding mirror neurons suggest that humans have the capacity to mimic the emotions of others. "The discovery of mirror neurons reveals that, often without our awareness, we are being influenced by the feelings state of others" (Uhl & Stuchul, 2011, p. 31). When teachers are joyful in their teaching, their students' neurons mimic that joy, and they become joyful students. When that happens and the focus is on joy, then productivity and learning increase. The field of positive psychology knows the importance of happiness and joy; it's time for education to recognize the importance of joy and put that focus into practice.

REFLECTION QUESTIONS

- How would you describe the "persona" of your school?
- Review the ten concepts presented by Wolk. What are you doing in your building to foster these concepts?
- What ceremonies occur in your building that celebrate staff and student success?
- What are the core beliefs of your school?
- In what ways do they breed a culture of joy?
- Reflect on the last time you created something not related to your school or classroom. How did it feel?
- How can you capture that feeling and translate it into learning experiences for teachers in your building?
- What does it mean to find pleasure in learning? Consider asking five teachers in your building what it means to find pleasure in learning.
- How are their responses different?

- How can you use this information to inform how you build and nurture a joyous culture in your building?
- How would you respond when there are moments where you are less joyous? List two or three strategies you can employ to reset yourself and the culture in the building.

REFERENCES

Achor, S. (2010). *The happiness advantage.* New York, NY: Crown Publishing Group.

Anderson, L. W., Krathwohl, D. R., Airasian, P. W., Cruikshank, K. A., Mayer, R. E., Pintrich, . . . Wittrock, M. C. (2001). *A taxonomy for learning, teaching, and assessing: A revision of Bloom's taxonomy of educational objectives, abridged edition.* White Plains, NY: Longman.

Carr, S., & Bryson, A. (2017). *Learning to love assessment: Unraveling complexities and generating solutions.* Lanham, MD: Rowman & Littlefield.

Greunert, S., & Whitaker, T. (2015). *School culture rewired: How to define, assess, and transform it.* Alexandria, VA: ASCD.

Habegger, S. (2008, September/October). The principal's role in successful schools: Creating a positive school culture. *Principal, 88*(1), 42–46.

Merriam-Webster. (n.d.). Joy. *Merriam-Webster.com.* Retrieved June 19, 2018, from www.merriamwebster.com/dictionary/joy

Peterson, K. (1994). *Building collaborative cultures: Seeking ways to reshape urban schools.* Naperville, IL: NCREL.

Pink, D. (2009). *Drive: The surprising truth about what motivates us.* New York, NY: Riverhead Books.

Ripp, P. (2017). Welcome to 7-0 English. *The adventures in Ms. Ripp's Class.* Blog post retrieved from www.mrsripp.com/2017/08

Robinson, K., & Aronica, L. (2015). *Creative schools: The grassroots revolution that's transforming education.* New York, NY: Penguin Books.

Uhl, C., & Stuchul, D. (2011). *Teaching as if life matters: The promise of a new education culture.* Baltimore, MD: Johns Hopkins University Press.

Whitaker, T. (2003). *What great principals do differently: Fifteen things that matter most.* Larchmont, NY: Eye on Education.

Wolk, S. (2008). Joy in school. *Educational Leadership, 66*(1), 8–15.

Chapter Four

Autonomy and Trust

Autonomy: The quality or state of being self-governing; self-directing freedom and especially moral independence.—Merriam-Webster.com

Trust: Assured reliance on the character, ability, strength, or truth of someone or something; one in which confidence is placed.—Merriam-Webster.com

The purpose of this chapter is to explore the role of a school leader, expressly an elementary principal, in creating a culture of autonomy and trust among teachers, particularly when teachers are presented with conflicting messages. As evidenced in chapter 1, policy, politics, and commodification have influenced how teachers see themselves as professionals. In fact, these three issues have impacted the expanding role of the principal.

The authors stress the difference between leadership and administration, but the authors also address the importance of leadership style and resultant management practices. Leadership and administration are not necessarily synonymous; having a high level of success and proficiency as an administrator (manager) does not necessarily make an individual a strong, effective leader.

LEADER VERSUS ADMINISTRATOR

A leader is one who has vision, communicates that vision, makes decisions aligned to the vision, but most of all, invests others in the vision. An elementary school leader must exhibit these qualities but also must be able to inspire teachers, students, families, and community. Jason, Margaret-Mary, and Tynisha believe there is a stark difference between a leader and an administrator. An elementary administrator is one who creates the schedule to ensure the first and third graders don't have art at the same time on the same day because the art room is too small. An elementary administrator is one who can review the quarterly budget to ensure they aren't overspending. An elementary administrator organizes the professional development activities for the school. A leader, however, is much more than an adept manager.

The draw of leadership is to be able to chart a course, define objectives, and invest in and motivate others. A leader sets the tone in which outcomes are defined and change occurs. Many educators aspire to leadership, specifically school leadership. Unlike many professions that have a promotional structure, schools operate differently. In order to seek promotion, one has to leave the classroom and then attain additional education and certification.

True leaders desire to make a difference in the lives of others; they are not just concerned about their own career trajectory. Many school leaders view their role as a vocation or as service. Sergiovanni (1996) explores servant leadership, claiming that the origins of school leadership are positioned in serving the common good and influenced by moral leadership.

Sergiovanni describes the two sources of authority on which school leaders base their practices: professional authority and moral authority. Professional authority leads teachers to expect and respond to collective socialization within a campus and to internal expertise within a faculty and to depend on an understanding of recommended practices. Moral authority is a comprehension of the obligations and duties derived from widely shared values and beliefs.

Under moral authority, teachers respond to genuine sharing of vision and commitment and, as a result, form a connection or bond of interdependence with one another within the school community. The strongest school leaders encapsulate these attributes—serving the common good of the school community with a focus on students and providing school leadership that is based on a moral sense of leadership. "The moral aspects of school leadership are important because schools function as extensions of families, and principals and teachers function *in loco parentis*"—in the place of a parent (Sergiovanni, 2000, p. 83).

Second to service for a school leader is the chance to create and establish a culture that reflects the leader's beliefs and vision. Beliefs, as described in chapter 2, are a difficult construct, as they are grounded in personal experiences. However, a literacy leader has the unique responsibility to have clarity in what effective literacy instruction looks like, to support teachers to become effective literacy teachers, and to celebrate literacy successes. As the authors note in chapter 2, it is not an easy feat because beliefs inform culture. And the principal's beliefs need to commingle with instructional staff's beliefs about teaching and learning.

Establishing a culture that reflects the leader's beliefs and vision may sound self-centered and egotistical. It is not meant to be; it is meant to be honest. A leader needs to both generate and nurture ideas, to marshal needed support and resources, and to facilitate through implementation. Sergiovanni (1992) defines *leadership* as inspiring others by either persuasion or example or by tapping into inner moral forces.

Making final decisions and ensuring a decision's follow-through is the role of the school leader. However, striving to achieve collaborative leadership is vital when seeking a viable solution or making a decision. School leaders, then, must have the autonomy to make the decisions they believe to be in the best interest of their school, staff, and most importantly their students. However, that is a simplified view of school leadership.

Exercising autonomy creates tension between professional authority and moral authority, or what a school leader believes is best for the school she is leading—including teachers, students, their families, and the school community—and what the district or perhaps the state mandates and requires. Every school leader the authors know experiences this tension.

School leadership, similar to any other leadership, is typically results-oriented. Principals, like other leaders, direct and manage by communicating the vision of the school district and working to make that vision reality. Sergiovanni (1996) claims that those who are successful pay close attention to both seeking out and nurturing people who will commit to this vision and assist it to fruition. However, district vision isn't always aligned with a school's vision or the beliefs of faculty. This calls into question how school leaders maneuver and negotiate between professional authority and moral authority and how this tension between the two kinds of authority impacts autonomy.

Autonomy sounds plausible in theory, but in reality, it is difficult to achieve. The authors suggest considering Sergiovanni in his discussion of building a covenant. Sergiovanni (1992) states, "When purpose, social contract, and local school autonomy becomes the basis of schooling, two important things happen. The school is transformed from an organization to a covenantal community, and the basis of authority changes from an emphasis on bureaucratic and psychological authority to moral authority" (p. 102). However, competing forces make autonomy complex, multifaceted, and difficult to achieve.

Autonomous decision-making assumes a high level of accountability both to those whom the school leader supervises and to those whom the school leader answers. In the case of literacy leadership, when a school leader's decisions do not result in meeting the objectives set forth by the school board and the superintendent, then a change in leadership is typically necessitated. But only responding to district mandates involving literacy can also negate the voices of teachers, students, their families, and the school community. This kind of dissonance illustrates the tension between moral authority and professional authority and directly influences autonomy.

The authors wonder how many school leaders would remain as school leaders if they were stripped of the autonomy to chart the course for their school. Their supposition: not many. Issues of local knowledge—that unique knowledge teachers and principals possess about their students, families, and the school community—can often compete with district mandates about literacy. The tension between moral authority and professional authority directly influences autonomy.

The authors postulate that school literacy leaders strive to have both the trust of the school board and superintendent and the trust of the teachers at their assigned campus as well as the autonomy in terms of decision-making to meet the demands of their school community. In the same way that school literacy leaders want both the trust that they will do their job and the autonomy to do it, in a similar manner then, it is fair to assume that teachers desire the same from their school leaders. Teachers want to be trusted that they have the literacy expertise, professionalism, literacy content, and literacy pedagogical knowledge to make informed classroom decisions. Teachers also want the autonomy to make decisions in the best interests of their students.

THE FAILED PROMISES OF AUTONOMY AND TRUST

If you are a literacy leader, reflect on your days as a teacher. How frequently did you hear "Teachers have a lot of flexibility" or "You have flexibility in how you teach, but not what you teach"? It's a saying that Tynisha, Margaret-Mary, and Jason often hear, and it makes sense. In some elementary buildings, it is true. These are the promises the authors were told, and they posit that some teachers are still being told, "You have flexibility." However, it appears that the increased push for a standardized curricular experience may be undermining "You have flexibility in how you teach."

In fact, Tynisha and Margaret-Mary remember their time as classroom teachers. Early in their teaching careers, their teacher mentors would tell them to shut their doors and just teach. To teach was to do what was best for kids, to meet their needs, to differentiate, and if you were not aligned to the scope and sequence, it was fine because you were meetings students' needs. Both Tynisha and Margaret-Mary were encouraged to refine their craft, teach what children needed, ensure that students loved coming to school, and make learning engaging. But as teacher educators, Tynisha and Margaret-Mary see many teachers who have been reduced to technicians, a description appearing with increasing frequency in educational literature within the last decade (Giroux, 2013; Kumashiro, 2010; Sleeter, 2008).

The tension that school leaders experience in trying to be autonomous literacy leaders is also keenly felt by many teachers who, as Sleeter (2008) explains, are compromised by economic forces. "External assaults that have their origins in global economic and political restructuring aim not only to de-professionalize teaching by devaluing professional preparation of teachers, but also to undermine equity and democracy by restructuring education around corporate needs" (p. 1947).

What also holds true is that every child should be guaranteed that during the course of a school year, he will be exposed to the same curricular standards, resources, and concepts as his peers in the neighboring classroom, school district, and state. That doesn't mean a restrictive, lock-step curriculum, but a curriculum rich in exposure to ideas and concepts, resources and skills, and engagement. If every teacher teaches whatever topic they want, whenever they want, schools also run the risk of having a disjointed curriculum that will have gaping holes for our students.

Pink (2009) stresses the importance of autonomy for professionals to experience happiness and effectiveness in their jobs. The reality of the promise of autonomy has failed in schools due to the enormity of expectations, the lack of professionalism offered teachers in the form of mandated commercial materials without the autonomy to implement as they determine is needed, a lack of respect for their profession, and an absence of trust. If the key to a student's success is the teacher in the classroom, then literacy leaders need to give teachers the support, autonomy, and trust to make the instructional decisions that are responsive to their students' needs while adhering to the spirit of a mandate. Anything less will result in mediocrity or worse: stagnation and unfulfilled teachers with disengaged students.

ENORMITY OF EXPECTATIONS

Unfortunately, the promise of autonomy is eroded by the enormity of expectations placed on elementary teachers and the powerful economic forces behind such expectations. Elementary teachers have a tough job. They build the foundation for all future learning. If the elementary teacher is unable to find a way to get his/her students to read by the end of their elementary career, the odds of the students ever catching up decline dramatically. In fact, research from the past several decades consistently illustrates that students who are behind in reading in early grades will also be behind in later grades (Graves, Juhl, & Graves, 2001; Juhl, 1988).

A typical elementary teacher's day includes as little as two preps: literacy and math. However, some elementary teachers may have as many as four core preps. Among the four preps are math, science, social studies, and literacy. On top of all of these tasks, there is keyboarding, technology, building inclusive classroom communities, as well as meeting the social and emotional needs of all elementary children entrusted to their care. In schools that serve low-income communities, second language learners, or students from traditionally marginalized groups, daily classroom routines may be even more challenging.

Prepping for literacy instruction, depending on the grade level, is not limited to explicit phonics instruction with repeated readings. Literacy instruction includes writing, spelling, and reading comprehension. When schools are teaching literacy as robust instruction, the literacy skills of listening, speaking, and viewing are also integrated and valued. Educators who chose to work in an elementary school recognize the number of required preparations and responsibilities that surface each day.

The focus on student performance on standardized tests as early as kindergarten creates a situation in which teachers—experts in the field of learning and child development—are now forced to introduce children to the stressors related to standardized testing. Teachers feel the stress acutely because failure of their students to show the expected growth on the standardized tests is increasingly tied to performance reviews. As this happens, a teacher's freedom to make autonomous and responsive instructional decisions based on appropriate developmental skills is seriously undermined as a result of inappropriate expectations.

Teacher stress is also felt by the school leader, the instructional leader, the literacy leader—the school principal. In many cases, the school principal received test scores over the summer and, prior to the return of teachers, thought long and hard about how to communicate the school's need to do better. Our system of providing feedback to principals has been grounded in intradistrict or interdistrict school comparisons. Regardless, the comparisons remind principals that they are not doing enough, and they need to improve.

The trickle-down message—from the media, politicians, commercial interests, and district administrators—is that teachers need to do better. Often, teachers are told to do the following in lockstep:

- simply follow the curriculum or scope and sequence;
- attend more data retreats; and
- implement more progress monitoring.

The result is the message that there needs to be less autonomy and more oversight. This stress robs teachers of the joy inherent in teaching.

PROFESSIONALISM

When the authors speak of professionalism, they do not see professionalism in teachers, administrators, or school board members as a problem. Their experience reveals that the overwhelming majority of educators are dedicated and highly committed to the students they serve. The lack of professionalism is in how the field of education and public education in general is portrayed and who makes the decisions about education and the standards (Schneider, 2014, 2015).

It is difficult to teach with autonomy if what you are being asked to teach is something in which you have had little input. The resources that teachers are given to deliver content are double-edged swords. In some ways, a resource is desirable, providing structure and guidance for teachers in how to deliver the expected content, especially for novices. In other ways, the resource is seen as a tool of efficiency.

For an extended and already-overworked elementary teacher, having a commercial resource that packages content may allow for more time to devote to all of the curricular areas. However, a reliance on a prepackaged resource seriously undermines the education profession as a whole, as the hidden message is that autonomy and reflexive teaching practices are not valued. According to the commercial program, all the ways to differentiate are located in the index or in the supplemental materials located in Book B of the resource. Programs do not teach, and no matter the caliber of a program, it is the teacher who can make the most precise instructional decisions. Decision-making and professional judgment are the joy of teaching.

For teachers, the reliance on the resource decreases responsiveness to the needs of students. Rather than addressing student needs, utilizing teachers' talent, expertise, and skill in making autonomous instructional decisions, teachers feel compelled to follow the resources, especially when pressured to do so. While the use of a resource is not inherently a bad thing, the unintended message is telling teachers they may not have the professionalism or decision-making skills to deliver the content without relying on the provided resource.

Additionally, teachers have a professional responsibility to continue to improve and question practices. While the majority of teachers are committed to lifelong learning and improving their craft, there are teachers who are comfortable teaching the same lessons the same way year after year, regardless of the academic needs of their class. Teachers who continue to do the same and choose not to change are not in abundance.

The authors have witnessed the ways in which teachers demonstrate their commitment to lifelong learning. They have seen teachers spend money out of their own pockets to support student learning and to refine their craft, such as paying to attend a conference or for professional development, because they want to increase skill and expertise as teachers. However, when a teacher chooses not to engage, then the consequence is evident. A strong literacy leader will see this quickly and have structures in places to support the teacher. If trust in a teacher has been compromised, then the school leader must intervene and potentially curtail that individual's autonomy.

TRUST

As literacy leaders, building principals, literacy coaches, classroom teachers, as people, we long for trust. Trust is part of the human condition. There's trust that teachers will do the right things for students. While we long for trust from others, we may not always trust ourselves. Not trusting in our own ability makes it hard to be autonomous in our teaching. As one teacher who works with Jason stated, "I want to have choice in what I teach. But sometimes it would just be easier if you would tell me what to teach." When asked why she felt that way, she followed up with, "Then I wouldn't have to worry about doing the wrong thing for my kids." "The wrong thing for my kids" is a powerful statement.

This is an exceptional, award-winning teacher, recognized for her expertise, and she doesn't trust herself. It is hard to expect students, parents, or community members to trust literacy leaders and teachers. The trust must be established first within the building and among instructional staff.

As professionals, we have allowed our trust to be slowly eradicated by reliance on commercial resources that prescribe on what day, at what time, and from what page we will be teaching. Teachers did not become teachers to instruct from a manual placed on their laps that constrains what they say as they teach. They became teachers to make a difference in the lives of their students. Award-winning teachers can contemplate doing the right things for their students; however, they cannot lose trust in themselves to make responsive and correct instructional decisions for their students. Responsiveness and astute instructional decision-making come with experience and support.

TIERED AUTONOMY AND TRUST

A first-year teacher is easy to spot. Just walk through an elementary building a few weeks before school starts. While teachers are not required to be working, undoubtedly the classrooms will be alive with activity as teachers prepare for the beginning of the school year. However, in the classroom of a first-year teacher, you will often find the teacher standing in the middle of the classroom with a look of "where do I begin?"

The "where do I begin?" look of new teachers also creeps into their instructional practices. The enthusiasm for teaching and making a difference in the lives of students radiates from new teachers. Therefore, it is the responsibility of the literacy leader to do the following:

- understand the curriculum;
- understand how to differentiate instruction;
- understand how to manage a classroom; and

- support a life/work balance culture that does not leave early career teachers feeling overwhelmed and exhausted.

Allowing teachers high levels of autonomy in their first year may not create a condition of success for them or their students. What they need in their first year is a tiered autonomy through strategic mentoring.

Tiered autonomy is defined as granting teachers increased autonomy as they demonstrate increasing ability to make effective instructional decisions that align with the needs of their students as well as with learning targets for their grade level and curricular area. Novice teachers may be required to use the district-selected resources as their guide. This can scaffold a novice's mastery of content and pacing the flow of a lesson and can remove some of the pressure to design and create learning experiences of their choosing. At this early point in their careers, new teachers lack the number of resources in their teaching "toolbox."

Therefore, allowing novice teachers unlimited autonomy may actually delay their professional development rather than encourage it. A tiered approach to instructional autonomy is not merely reserved for new teachers. Additionally, veteran teachers may also experience more restrictive autonomy if they have been unable to demonstrate a clear understanding of students' needs or curricular objectives.

If teachers, regardless of length of service, fail to meet instructional, curricular, and socioemotional needs of students, then they do not deserve the luxury of implementing autonomous instructional decision-making. In such instances, mentors and literacy coaches can scaffold support through observations with feedback, demonstration lessons, and lesson-planning assistance. A literacy leader facilitates this kind of support.

While it may sound harsh, teachers must demonstrate they are able to make good decisions that are reflective of the needs of their students, are based on recommended practices, and show student achievement. This is not unlike asking students in their classrooms to demonstrate success. In many ways the tiered approach to teacher autonomy is correlated with the gradual release model. A literacy leader has to facilitate and monitor both autonomy and support. Teachers' levels of autonomous instructional behavior do not necessarily reflect that they are either effective or ineffective teachers. The more autonomous teachers can be within their classroom, the more joyful learning and teaching will occur.

TEACHER AUTONOMY, TRUST, AND THE IMPACT ON THE SCHOOL LEADER

Creating a school culture built on trust and teacher autonomy may be a Herculean feat. In some cases, a school literacy leader may find it easier to mandate that every teacher follow the manual, scope and sequence, or teacher's edition without exception. Tynisha taught in a school where the school leader demanded that each teacher in the specific grade level be on the same page of the text and use the student practice materials and assessments. There was no trust and, therefore, no autonomy.

In this mindset, the school leader assumed that all teachers will teach the same content in the same way and that all students will receive the same educational experience. With increased political influence, curricular mandates, and parent expectations and with less and less time to meet those expectations, the lure of a nonautonomous framework for teachers may be hard to ignore. This model will not create the conditions in which teachers, students, or school leaders experience deep, rigorous, joyful, and meaningful learning. In fact, it creates conditions in which the focus becomes student test scores, getting through content, and removing joy from the learning experience.

In creating a culture where teachers have an increased sense of autonomy and joy, the school leader must commit to being visible. The role shifts from evaluator to supporter, collaborator, coach, and motivator. There is a huge expectation and historical tradition for the school leader being the instructional leader of the school. That is important but, in many ways, unrealistic.

A school literacy leader cannot be an expert in all curricular areas or an expert in all classroom-management strategies. The literacy leader is a learner alongside his or her teachers. The literacy leader facilitates the literacy vision and sets the course of the school. The teachers make literacy learning happen. A school literacy leader can make teachers more joyful, autonomous, and effective by being the following:

- supporter;
- collaborator; and
- motivator.

Supporter

To create a trusting and autonomous culture, a school literacy leader must support teachers. This means supporting them in their risk-taking. When teachers want to try something new, a literacy leader listens, finds ways to say yes, and provides them the resources to be successful. This means also putting your own worries aside. The risk may result in failure.

Failure is learning, and teachers grow through failure. The school literacy leader must walk with teachers through their journeys to autonomy by providing the ideas, research, resources, and support to make them stronger at their craft. The school literacy leader must also be willing to take risks and make their risk-taking visible to teachers and students. If they are to be the lead learners and instructional literacy leaders of the school, a strong sense of support comes through modeling their expectations.

Collaborator

To achieve an autonomous and trusting school culture, the school literacy leader must collaborate with teachers. While a major role of the school literacy leader is that of an evaluator and supervisor, this role can be achieved by collaborating with teachers. A classroom teacher must work to grow each student. A school literacy leader must view his/her role as a collaborator who focuses on teacher growth rather than an evaluator who focuses on artificial rubrics and, once or twice a year, dog-and-pony-show observations and evaluations. To be a collaborator, the school literacy leader needs to model learning alongside the teachers. That means working to create lessons with them and actually teaching the lessons alongside them.

This level of collaboration is both time-intensive and demands teaching expertise. It is also scary as hell for the school literacy leader, but the benefits outweigh the anxiety. Working and learning alongside teachers creates a culture in which the school literacy leader trusts the decision-making process of teachers and the teachers trust the shared vision and supervision of the school literacy leader. Sitting in the office and simply trusting that things are going well is ineffective and a dereliction of a school leader's moral responsibility to teachers and students.

Motivator

To create autonomy and trust, a school literacy leader must be a motivator. Teaching in an elementary school is rewarding beyond compare, but it is equally exhausting. Motivating instructional staff to continue to believe in the benefits of autonomy in their literacy instruction practices results in higher levels of satisfaction. To accomplish this, the school literacy leader must make it a priority to visit classrooms daily.

The literacy leader must talk with the students, be present, and observe the amazing things that teachers accomplish. Literacy leaders create autonomy by both supporting and modeling literacy in myriad ways as support: They read aloud to students and listen as students read to them. They comment on displayed writing as well as write to and with students. Such supportive behavior serves to motivate teachers.

Letting your teachers know you are interested in what they do serves as a tremendous motivator. Just visiting without feedback is not enough. Literacy leaders need to create ways to communicate about what they observe and experience while visiting classrooms. Consider the following: Leave a hand-written note, even if it is just a "gumdrop and lollipop" note. Remember, this job is exhausting; getting a handwritten note is a far greater motivator than an email or note in a file. Comment on specific literacy practices you observe and that align with the shared vision.

Autonomy is a challenging, time-consuming, and exhausting construct for school leaders. But it's worth it. When teachers reclaim the autonomy and joy in their classrooms, they become joyful, and they feel fulfilled. More importantly, learning becomes a joyful process that leaves students engaged and wanting more each day.

The purpose of this chapter was to address the failed promises of autonomy within school culture. Tynisha, Jason, and Margaret-Mary have a deep understanding of the role of standards, testing, and accountability. This chapter shed light on how these constructs can cloud the ability of a principal who is a literacy leader to lead from a place to trust. The work of a literacy leader means there are opportunities for teachers to experience autonomy. The authors described a tiered approach to creating an autonomous culture where trust sits at the core. Finally, the authors explored reasons why joy and autonomy can be difficult to achieve. Chapter 5 provides a unique perspective on decision-making and professionalizing the teaching profession.

REFLECTION QUESTIONS

- How would you describe yourself: Are you more of an administrator or a leader?
- How would you articulate your vision?
- How would you rally teachers, staff, students, and families around your vision?
- Where have you seen joy exemplified in your building?
- Who are the teachers in your building who feel that they have autonomy?
- What are the characteristics of these teachers, and what does teaching look like in their classrooms?
- Why do you think they feel autonomous?

REFERENCES

Giroux, H. A. (2013). Neoliberalism's war against teachers in dark times. *Cultural Studies? Critical Methodologies, 13*(6), 458–468.

Graves, M. F., Juel, C., & Graves, B. B. (2001). *Teaching reading in the 21st century* (2nd ed.). Boston, MA: Allyn and Bacon.

Juel, C. (1988). Learning to read and write: A longitudinal study of 54 children from first through fourth grades. *Journal of Educational Psychology, 80,* 437–447.

Kumashiro, K. K. (2010). Seeing the bigger picture: Troubling movements to end teacher education. *Journal of Teacher Education, 61*(1–2), 56–65.

Merriam-Webster. (n.d.). Autonomy. *Merriam-Webster.com.* Retrieved June 19, 2018, from www.merriam-webster.com/dictionary/autonomy.

Merriam-Webster. (n.d.). Trust. *Merriam-Webster.com.* Retrieved June 19, 2018, from www.merriam-webster.com/dictionary/trust.

Pink, D. (2009). *Drive: The surprising truth about what motivates us.* New York, NY: Riverhead.

Schneider, M. (2014). *A chronicle of echoes: Who's who in the implosion of American public education.* Charlotte, NC: Information Age.

Schneider, M. (2015). *Common core dilemma: Who owns our schools.* New York, NY: Teachers College Press.

Sergiovanni, T. J. (1992). *Moral leadership: Getting to the heart of school improvement.* San Francisco, CA: Jossey-Bass.

Sergiovanni, T. J. (1996). *Leadership for the schoolhouse: How is it different? Why is it important?* San Francisco, CA: Jossey-Bass.

Sergiovanni, T. J. (2000). *The lifeworld of leadership: Creating culture, community, and personal meaning in our schools.* The Jossey-Bass Education Series. San Francisco, CA: Jossey-Bass.

Sleeter, C. (2008). Equity, democracy, and neoliberal assaults on teacher education. *Teaching and Teacher Education, 24*(8), 1947–1957.

Chapter Five

Professionalism and Decision-Making

In previous chapters, Tynisha, Margaret-Mary, and Jason have attempted to define the complex, complicated, and multifaceted role of an elementary principal. As the literacy leader, an elementary principal is the individual chiefly responsible for implementing a school's mission and vision (Hallinger & Heck, 2002), the person facilitating instructional leadership (Booth & Rowsell, 2007; Hallinger, 2003; Hallinger & Murphy, 1985; Zepeda, 2007), and the primary person responsible for supporting faculty through astute supervision and management (Leithwood, Louis, Anderson, & Wahlstrom, 2004). In this chapter, the authors shift the focus from the principal as literacy leader and a campus's chief decision-maker to teachers as decision-makers within classrooms.

In order to facilitate collective and individual faculty beliefs into coherent, shared practices, the elementary literacy leader also assumes responsibility for acquiring literacy funds of knowledge that guide his or her supervision and management and result in enhanced student outcomes. As well, the literacy leader must also establish and sustain a school culture that allows for the implementation of mission, vision, and beliefs (Sergiovanni, 2000). The elementary literacy leader must likewise satisfy students' families and the school community. Promoting, guiding, and facilitating teacher decision-making is part of a literacy leader's responsibility.

The authors have deliberated over the pressures placed on an elementary principal—the literacy leader of the campus. The accountability movement in the United States, of which standardized testing, scripted curricula, and narrow, prescriptive teaching are emblematic (Schneider, 2016; Sleeter, 2008), is one kind of pressure felt by an elementary literacy leader. In tandem with accountability are the political pressures and resultant policies that can constrain literacy leadership at the elementary level (Allington, 2002, 2004;

Altwerger, 2005; Bomer, 2005), whether the pressure is brought to bear by those who directly manage principals, or by school boards, state superintendents of education, the policies and dictums of the U.S. Department of Education, or commercial interests driving the commodification of education (Apple, 2012).

Accountability, political pressures, and the pressure experienced when corporate interests shaping education collide place intense pressure on elementary literacy leaders and classroom teachers as well as any educator supporting instruction. In fact, these pressures and resultant tensions are increasing, particularly in public schools. What the literacy leader and his or her faculty believe is best for the children entrusted to them may be at odds with outside interests.

Unfortunately, the expectations to respond to these pressures are placed squarely on elementary literacy leaders. These myriad pressures are additionally exacerbated by the tensions that result from the conflict that principals may experience between assuming professional authority and shouldering moral authority (Sergiovanni, 1992). The pressures and tension faced by elementary literacy leaders are further aggravated by the perceived loss of autonomy. Layered on these pressures are the historical traditions of U.S. education—traditions slow to change and continually influencing teaching and learning.

Teacher decision-making is directly tied to the type of leadership an elementary principal elects to implement. In a shared instructional model, suggested by Printy, Mark, and Bowers (2009), instructional leadership results in improved quality of instruction, appropriate and child-centered curricular choices, and assessment practices that reflect quality pedagogical practices. Ultimately, this kind of leadership increases student outcomes and achievement. As discussed in chapter 1, the elementary literacy leader sets the tone for shared faculty responsibility, integrated instructional leadership, and ultimately, judicious teacher decision-making in the classroom.

HISTORICAL PERSPECTIVES OF U.S. EDUCATION: A BRIEF SYNOPSIS

Schooling in the United States has undergone several iterations from the beginning as a privilege reserved for wealthy White males when the United States was a young country. Schooling then evolved to represent a factory model that was prevalent in the 1900s and was a highly segregated system. Segregation was addressed by U.S. society during the 1950s and through the 1970s. Contemporary models are a result of the seemingly inclusive free public education model touted after the passage of Public Law 94-142. In fact, public education in the United States has long been tied to democracy and economics, but not always extended to all segments of U.S. society.

Based on the premise that an educated populace equates to a capable workforce, education serves society. The factory model (Dolence & Norris, 1995; Johnson, 2010; Leland & Kasten, 2011; Rose, 2012; Serafini, 2011) regarded children as products; hence, the school was conceived as an educational factory complete with rows of desks, the formation of lines, uniformity of instruction, grade placement based solely on birthdays, and a production mentality. Thus, standardized testing turned into the quality-control mechanism for measuring educational progress (Leland & Kasten, 2011).

Economic production during and after WWII impacted education in significant and lasting ways by furthering the factory model of education. The factory model of education (Dolence & Norris, 1995; Rose, 2012; Serafini, 2011) promoted sameness, uniformity, and homogeneity and emphasized processes and products versus outputs—what some have referred to as "cookie-cutter" teaching and learning. Rapid advances in technology, mass communication, and digital ways of communicating and transmitting information have replaced how we think of education but not necessarily pedagogical practices. What educators and economists call the Information Age replaced the last vestiges of the Industrial Age. Dolence and Norris (1995) claim that "the 1990s mark the first decade of the Information Age" (p. 6).

Over two decades prior to the publication of this volume, Dolence and Norris (1995) posited several fundamental questions regarding the transition from Industrial Age to Information Age models of teaching. They wrote:

> Three simple questions must be answered by political leaders, educational leaders, faculty, students, and other stakeholders contemplating the future of higher education. First, "Is today's Industrial Age educational model appropriate to the learning needs of the Information Age—for either traditional learners or learners in the workplace?" Second, "Is society willing to pay for a 20th century 'Industrial Age' model in the 21st century 'Information Age?'" And third, "Can academe afford to miss the opportunity of reshaping itself to serve the emerging needs of the Information Age learner?" (p. 12)

Although aimed at the future of higher education, Dolence and Norris questioned whether the learning needs of students could be met with outdated transmission models of teaching in the collegiate arena; this same argument holds true for elementary-aged students.

The authors of this volume ask questions similar to Dolence and Norris. For instance, can elementary teachers afford to continue to teach whole-group configurations as a primary literacy instructional practice? We also wonder: Is the implementation of English language arts standards serving the needs of today's elementary students in terms of literacy acquisition? And, we ask: Is the notion of "the literacy core," and subsequent tiered literacy instruction, often merely different commercial approaches to core literacy concepts, mindful of the differentiation needed to ensure all elementary-aged children emerge with twenty-first-century literacy skills?

Finally, we ask, is economic impetus driving literacy practice? What is the impact on the teaching profession, the morale of teachers, and ultimately, students? Mammoth publishing companies such as Pearson are driving educational decision-making, stripping teachers of the ability to use their expertise in seeking appropriate materials. Basal readers, which emerged during WWI and served an historical purpose of providing guidance to novice and less-skilled educators, are often touted as "the literacy curriculum," but in reality, they de-skill teachers (Baumann, 1992; Chall & Squire, 1996; Dewitz & Jones, 2013; Shannon, 1987, 1989).

Goodman (1986) was an early vocal opponent of the singular use of textbook over teacher decision-making, claiming that "textbooks lagged behind the best knowledge in the field they represent" (p. 358). In some school systems and campuses, test-prep marketers drive instructional choice, often in the entire semester of state testing.

The factory model of education has resulted in a factory model of teaching wherein all students master the same concepts utilizing rote learning methods. The factory model conjures images of desks in straight rows, silent classrooms, sameness, repetitiveness, and monotony. The factory model is a perfect fit for standardized testing and commercial literacy programs that emphasize uniformity. As authors, we reflect: Has the factory model of education given rise to and caused a factory model of teaching? In chapter 4, Tynisha shared a time in her teaching career when she experienced this kind of teaching wherein she was not allowed any autonomy in decision-making.

Elementary teachers and literacy leaders recognize that this mode of learning and assessment does little to foster creativity and meet the ever-changing demands of twenty-first-century literacy. But the factory model and the use of economics as a driver of educational policy and practice persists. However, the shift in an economic basis for education has been from what is good for the country and what promotes democracy to what is profitable for business while restricting access for many segments of U.S. society. Both the factory model and educational commodification rob elementary teachers and elementary literacy leaders of autonomy in curriculum and pedagogy. Education is currently perceived as a market; teachers are factory workers and technicians, and students and their families are clients.

ECONOMICS, POLITICS, AND EDUCATION: EROSION OF TEACHER DECISION-MAKING

A prime example of how education has traditionally served society in terms of economics is the original Elementary and Secondary Education Act (ESEA; 1965). Passed by Congress on April 1, 1965, during the height of the U.S. Civil Rights Movement, ESEA was designed to provide equal access to education. Increased access to education was perceived as a way to also increase economic stability. For many segments of U.S. society, equal access was hidden behind the "separate but equal" doctrine outlawed by the landmark legislate of *Brown v. Board of Education* (1954). While ESEA was hopeful and promised to address inequity regarding resources, opportunity, and teacher quality, subsequent reauthorizations have not held this promise.

A significant reauthorization of ESEA was No Child Left Behind (NCLB; 2001). However, NCLB relied on "factory models of education, business paradigms, and conservative ideology" (Johnson, 2010, p. 34). While NCLB was touted as being based on scientifically based research, that was not the case.

NCLB intensified personal and political forces (Allington, 2004; Garan, 2002, 2004; Shannon, 2007), determining the types of literacy instruction public school children receive, narrowing curriculum, and teaching to the content presented by a state, high-stakes test. Increasing mandates derived from NCLB (2001) dictated how educators teach. The literacy instruction "forced" on teachers in many cases negated teacher decision-making and did little to foster creativity or provide access to societal power for children (Finn, 1999; Gallagher, 2009; Meyer, 2010).

Sadly, corporate interests and the commodification of education were played out in this law, requiring certain kinds of literacy education that stymied creativity of both students and teachers, restricted the kinds of literacy experiences poor children and children of color received, and financially rewarded commercial literacy interests. Driven by accountability, NCLB failed millions of students in elementary schools and their teachers.

According to Johnson (2010), "Much of what is done in literacy education today reflects the philosophy of the industrial (or factory) model of education, which evolved during the late nineteenth and early twentieth centuries" (p. 34). In moments of reflection, when faced with difficult decisions regarding teacher education, and being literacy leaders, Tynisha, Jason, and Margaret-Mary ruminate if U.S. society would accept medicine rooted in the philosophy of the Industrial Age.

According to Serafini (2011), factory models of education prevalent in the 1900s have had a significant and long-term influence on U.S. educational curriculum, teaching methods, and testing frameworks. The effects of these structures can currently be seen in U.S. public schools. Ravitch and Kohn

(2014) claim, "Teachers are demoralized by the deskilling caused by federal policy" (p. vii).

But reducing the effects of standardized testing requires changes in teacher preparation programming, in the ways schools are organized, in mandated curriculum frameworks, and especially, in the methods of assessment currently used in public schools (Ravitch & Kohn, 2014). And viewing assessment as "reflective inquiry" rather than as a measurement of amassed facts also requires time, effort, a renewed perspective, and dialogue among educators, especially elementary literacy teachers and the elementary principals, like Jason, who led them.

Leland and Kasten (2011) extend Serafini's argument that the factory model of education is counterproductive to U.S. education, claiming the democracy required in the twenty-first century demands a citizenry "able to think critically and use learning and language flexibly to construct knowledge in a number of ways and contexts" (p. 5). Leland and Kasten (2011) argue that inquiry models of learning and teaching assist children with questioning their world, encourage critical thinking, and demand language that is flexible to learners and selected modes of inquiry. Further, they postulate that inquiry learning also promotes choice, creativity, and engagement—twenty-first-century literacy constructs (Leland & Kasten, 2011).

Like NCLB, the Every Student Succeeds Act (ESSA) (2016) has resulted in many teaching and learning scenarios that strip teachers of decision-making autonomy. As federal policy trickles down to states, districts, and school campuses, because of a preoccupation with formulaic, packaged, scripted curricula and high-stakes tests, teacher voices are effectively silenced and creativity is stifled, especially in the high-stakes discipline-specific area of literacy (Allington, 2002, 2004; Altwerger, 2005; Coles, 2003; Garan, 2002, 2004; Goodman, 1986; Johnson & Johnson, 2002).

WHY TEACHER DECISION-MAKING IS ESSENTIAL

The unpredictability of how the future may be shaped, such as advances in technology-driven information systems and platforms, digital environments, modes of transportation, and communication methods, makes it increasingly difficult to teach and to prepare teachers to teach. In the United States, education has taken many forms and paths, but as Darling-Hammond, Rothman, and Cookson (2017) remind us, the purpose of U.S. education should remain focused on students preparing for participation in democratic society: "The goals of our education system include improving student learning opportunities, strengthening educational attainment, providing alternatives that fit student needs, and integrating our diverse citizenry, while preparing young people for their civic roles in a democracy" (p. v).

Noddings (2005) asserts that schools and formal public education were created for moral and social reasons as well as for academic instruction. She further prompts us that students are whole persons whose learning should be connected versus compartmentalized. In elementary schools, the whole child is emphasized (Yoder, 2014). Language learning is interconnected and inter-related.

Learning to speak and learning to listen don't occur as isolated speech events. Learning occurs in a social context; thus, learning to read and write is similar (Goodman, 1989; Goodman & Goodman, 2014). Teachers, then, with principal support, need to find ways to teach literacy as rich, meaningful, and interconnected learning. According to Sir Ken Robinson (2006), despite the human capacity for creativity, schools in the twenty-first century have de-emphasized creativity of instruction.

Noddings (2005) claims, "In a democratic society, schools must go be-yond teaching fundamental skills" (p. 3). While this is easy to state, it is becoming harder and harder to accomplish. Teachers need to facilitate learning by being both instructional leaders as well as instructional decision-makers. In the same way that a principal assumes literacy leadership by having an instructional vision for a school campus and enacts this vision through a shared instructional model, teachers then, by extension, have instructional vision for their classrooms. In tandem with students, families, and communities, they enact their vision in a shared manner.

No matter the quality of a literacy curriculum, teachers teach students, not materials. It is teachers who know their students, families, and communities and are best positioned to make instructional, curricular, and pedagogical decisions. It is the literacy leader's role to recognize this and support his or her teachers in this capacity.

TRUSTING TEACHERS: LITERACY LEADERSHIP ENACTED

In earlier chapters, the authors touched on all the elements that make an effective literacy leader on a school campus. In the classroom, it is the teacher who utilizes the skills and knowledge regarding effective curriculum and pedagogical practices and knowledge of their students. Therefore, teachers should also select some forms of assessment to guide their differentiated instructional decision-making. However, a literacy leader needs to provide guidance, feedback, and trust for a teacher to do so. A literacy leader needs to trust the decisions regarding what teachers do in their classrooms. The teacher is the expert in the room—trust that!

Trust can be a hard commodity to give freely to teachers. There is so much accountability from local, state, and federal levels that literacy leaders take risks when they trust freely. Jason still struggles with this when he visits classrooms. For example, he may observe a teacher completing a project, allowing his or her students extra free time, or spending what would appear to be too much time on a mini-lesson or a read-aloud. He then remembers that he trusts his teachers.

There is a reason they have made an instructional decision. Just as his superintendent trusts him to make decisions that are in the best interest of Jason's school, Jason must trust his teachers in the same manner. Trust is hard to earn. Jason has found that by trusting his teachers to make all their decisions from the student-advocacy perspective, his teachers enjoy teaching more. He has also found that students are more engaged in the classroom because the teachers are trusted to be responsive to the needs of students.

In order to build trust, a literacy leader needs to facilitate dialog about teaching and learning, about curriculum and pedagogy, and about decision-making. At times, the authors want to tell elementary principals to "get over yourselves!" We don't mean this harshly; rather, a literacy leader—no matter how skilled and well-liked—cannot run a school single-handedly. They need teacher input, and they need to dispense trust liberally. A literacy leader needs to be able to recognize effective literacy instruction and recommended literacy practice. Becoming an elementary principal is not merely a career move. Collectively, the authors view it as a sacred trust and a heavy responsibility.

We do not want to oversimplify this process of trust-building. However, we also think it is simple. Our formula is as follows:

- Observe often.
- Talk to your teachers to gain understanding before judging their decision-making.
- Facilitate discussion and dialogue around literacy issues and decisions.
- Plan professional development that is strategic and specific and meets teachers' individual needs as well as collective needs.
- Keep it student-centered.
- Discuss literacy research often; it changes constantly.
- Meet district mandates judiciously.

We invite readers to take these seven points and implement them. Record what happens, and make this plan customized to your setting, students, teachers, and school community. Margaret-Mary lives by a saying she used when she was an assistant superintendent, responsible for over twenty-six thousand children on sixty-four campuses. She uses it now as a teacher educator: "If your decision is not in the best interest of students, don't do it." Again, easy to state but most difficult to enact, especially when pressured to do otherwise. The pressure can be intense, almost suffocating, pressure that eradicates joy and eliminates autonomy.

FINAL THOUGHTS

The social and political intent to deprofessionalize teaching and de-skill teachers is real, and it is demoralizing. Acknowledge these forces, read and learn about them, but at the very least, "talk back" against them. Stand up for the teachers assigned to your campus. Remind them often that *they are professionals*. Tynisha, Jason, and Margaret-Mary maintain that teaching is highly political, and politics often promotes commercial interests. Dialogues about the pressures, policies, and politics of education are hard but healthy discussions.

Being a good listener is crucial, but rants about teaching, mandates, and children are unacceptable and unproductive. When Margaret-Mary was an assistant superintendent, she often found herself listening to elementary principals complaining about issues. After a brief period of time, she made it clear that any issue, problem, or challenge brought to her also needed possible solutions.

This simple strategy allowed for issues to be brought to the forefront and addressed. Requiring solutions also made discussions about issues more productive. Additionally, asking for solutions engaged elementary principals under her supervision in shared solution-seeking and shared decision-making. Principals knew their ideas were valued. Maybe they weren't always the final solution, but the simple acts of listening and exploring solutions together were powerful and built mutual trust.

Finally, advocate for your teachers. If you don't, no one will.

Upon reflection as authors, after co-writing this chapter, we felt this chapter reads as a call to arms. Although that wasn't our original intent, it may be perceived as such. So be it. When we are discussing teachers as professionals, we can connect the teaching profession to other professions.

As Jason discussed with his co-authors,

> I think about when I go to a mechanic or have a contractor do work on my home—I trust them because they have a specialty, expertise, and knowledge that I don't possess. If they tell me I need something done, I trust them, and I do it. Now, I also check credentials and ask for references. Why do we not share that same thought about teachers' decisions and the teaching profession? Their opinions seem to be minimized rather than valued.

Both Tynisha and Margaret-Mary agreed.

The issues around deprofessionalizing teaching as a profession and the de-skilling of teachers are complex, ugly, and hard to discuss and consider. The authors have chosen to equip themselves with knowledge and remain as current as possible. Knowledge is power and, if used carefully, can be a formidable defense against the attacks on teaching and the teaching profession. How to wield that knowledge and power can be tricky. You have to pick your battles carefully—you want to remain employed yet always want to advocate for students and teachers. Jason's book studies are good examples of learning about recommended practice.

Reading and discussing recommended practice about literacy can serve to bring faculty together around important issues. Political readings are another avenue of professional reading and discussions. The authors highly recommend Mercedes Schneider's work: *A Chronicle of Echoes: Who's Who in the Implosion of American Public Education* (2014), *Common Core Dilemma: Who Owns Our Schools?* (2015), and *School Choice: The End of Public Education?* (2016). Schneider is a meticulous researcher who has found the courage to write about the issues and pressures facing public education. She is a provocative author, a high school English teacher, and an educator who has found her voice regarding the de-skilling of teachers and the attacks on public education.

Professional decision-making is explored in this chapter. The role of the literacy leader as it relates to instructional decision-making requires a culture of trust. Teachers must be seen as professionals who know their content, the craft, and most importantly their students. Chapter 6 extends this conversation within the context of culture. Culture is nuanced. Literacy culture has not been explored much in current literacy research. Literacy culture is discussed in the following chapter with special attention given to when breaches occur.

REFLECTION QUESTIONS

- Why have we chosen certain curricula?
- Why have we chosen certain pedagogical methods?
- Why have we chosen certain classroom arrangements?
- Why have we chosen certain learning objectives?
- As a literacy leader, how have you built a culture of trust among teachers?

REFERENCES

Allington, R. (2002). *Big brother and the national reading curriculum: How ideology trumped evidence.* Portsmouth, NH: Heinemann.
Allington, R. (2004, March). Setting the record straight. *Educational Leadership,* 22–25.
Altwerger, B. (2005). *Reading for profit.* Portsmouth, NH: Heinemann.
Apple, M. W. (2012). *Education and power.* New York, NY: Routledge.
Baumann, J. F. (1992). Commentary: Basal reading programs and the deskilling of teachers: A critical examination of the argument. *Reading Research Quarterly, 27*(4), 390–398.
Bomer, R. (2005). Missing the children: When politics and programs impede our teaching. *Language Arts, 82,* 168–176.
Booth, D., & Rowsell, J. (2007). *The literacy principal, leading, supporting, and assessing reading and writing initiatives* (2nd ed.). Portland, ME: Stenhouse.
Brown v. Board of Education, 347 U.S. 483, 74 S. Ct. 686, 98 L. Ed. 873 (1954).

Chall, J. S., & Squire, J. R. (1996). Industry the publishing and textbooks. *Handbook of Reading Research, 2*, 120.

Coles, G. (2003). *Reading: The naked truth*. Portsmouth, NH: Heinemann.

Darling-Hammond, L., Rothman, R., & Cookson, P. W., Jr. (2017). *Expanding high-quality educational options for all students: How states can create a system of schools worth choosing*. Palo Alto, CA: Learning Policy Institute.

Dewitz, P., & Jones, J. (2013). Using basal readers: From dutiful fidelity to intelligent decision making. *The Reading Teacher, 66*(5), 391–400.

Dolence, M., & Norris, D. M. (1995). *Transforming higher education*. Ann Arbor, MI: Society for College and University Planning.

Elementary and Secondary Education Act. (1965). *Public Law No. 89-10; 79 Stat. 27, 1965*. One hundred seventh Congress of the United States of America.

Every Student Success Act. (2016). *Public Law No. 114-95*. One hundred fourteenth Congress of the United States of America.

Finn, P. (1999). *Literacy with an attitude*. Albany, NY: State University of NY Press.

Gallagher, K. (2009). *Readicide*. Portland, ME: Stenhouse.

Garan, E. (2002). *Resisting reading mandates*. Portsmouth, NH: Heinemann.

Garan, E. (2004). *In defense of our children*. Portsmouth, NH: Heinemann.

Goodman, K. S. (1986). Basal readers: A call for action. *Language Arts, 63*(4), 358–363.

Goodman, K. S. (1989). Whole-language research: Foundations and development. *The Elementary School Journal, 90*(2), 207–221.

Goodman, Y. M., & Goodman, K. S. (2014). Vygotsky in a whole language perspective. In *Making sense of learners making sense of written language* (pp. 98–114). New York, NY: Routledge.

Hallinger, P. (2003). Leading educational change: Reflections on the practice of instructional and transformational leadership. *Cambridge Journal of Education, 33*(3), 329–351. doi:10.1080/0305764032000122005

Hallinger, P., & Heck, R. H. (2002). What do we call people with vision? The role of vision, mission and goals in school leadership and improvement. In K. A. Leithwood (Ed.), *Second international handbook of educational leadership and administration* (pp. 9–40). Dordrecht; Boston, MA: Kluwer.

Hallinger, P., & Murphy, J. (1985). Assessing the instructional management behavior of principals. *Elementary School Journal, 86*(2), 217–247.

Johnson, A. P. (2010). No Child Left Behind: Factory models and business paradigms. *The Clearing House: A Journal of Educational Strategies, Issues and Ideas, 80*(1), 34–36.

Johnson, D., & Johnson, B. (2002). *High stakes*. New York, NY: Rowman & Littlefield.

Leithwood, K. A., Louis, K. S., Anderson, S., & Wahlstrom, K. (2004). *How leadership influences student learning: Review of research*. Toronto, Canada: Center of Applied Research and Educational Improvement; Ontario Institute for Studies in Education, University of Toronto.

Leland, C., & Kasten, W. (2011). Literacy education for the 21st century: It's time to close the factory. *Reading & Writing Quarterly, 18*(1), 5–15.

Meyer, R. (2010). *Official portraits and unofficial counter portraits of "at-risk" students*. New York, NY: Routledge, Taylor & Francis.

No Child Left Behind. (2001). *Public Law No. 107-1110, 115 Stat. 1425, 2002*. One hundred seventh Congress of the United States of America.

Noddings, N. (2005). What does it mean to educate the whole child? *Educational Leadership, 63*(1), 3–11.

Printy, S. M., Marks, H. M., & Bowers, A. J. (2009). Integrated leadership: How principals and teachers share transformational and instructional influence. *Journal of School Leadership, 19*(5), 504–532.

Ravitch, D., & Kohn, A. (2014). *More than a score: The new uprising against high-stakes testing*. Chicago, IL: Haymarket Books.

Robinson, K. (2006). *Do schools kill creativity?* TED. Retrieved from www.ted.com/talks/ken_robinson_says_schools_kill_creativity

Rose, J. (2012). How to break free of our 19th-century factory-model education system. *The Atlantic, 9.*

Schneider, M. K. (2014). *A chronicle of echoes: Who's who in the implosion of American public education.* Charlotte, NC: Information Age Publishing.

Schneider, M. K. (2015). *Common core dilemma: Who owns our schools?* New York, NY: Teachers College Press.

Schneider, M. K. (2016). *School choice: The end of public education?* New York, NY: Teachers College Press.

Serafini, F. (2011). Dismantling the factory model of assessment. *Reading & Writing Quarterly, 18*(1), 67–85.

Sergiovanni, T. J. (1992). *Moral leadership: Getting to the heart of school improvement.* San Francisco, CA: Jossey-Bass.

Sergiovanni, T. J. (2000). *The lifeworld of leadership: Creating culture, community, and personal meaning in our schools.* The Jossey-Bass Education Series. San Francisco, CA: Jossey-Bass.

Shannon, P. (1987). Commercial reading materials, a technological ideology, and the deskilling of teachers. *The Elementary School Journal, 87*(3), 307–329.

Shannon, P. (1989). *Broken promises: Reading instruction in twentieth-century America.* Granby, MA: Bergin & Garvey.

Shannon, P. (2007). *Reading against democracy: The broken promises of reading instruction.* Portsmouth, NH: Heinemann.

Sleeter, C. (2008). Equity, democracy, and neoliberal assaults on teacher education. *Teaching and Teacher Education, 24*(8), 1947–1957.

Yoder, N. (2014). Teaching the whole child: Instructional practices that support social-emotional learning in three teacher evaluation frameworks. Research-to-Practice Brief. *Center on Great Teachers and Leaders.*

Zepeda, S. J. (2007). *The principal as instructional leader: A handbook for supervisors.* Larchmont, NY: Eye on Education.

Chapter Six

Culture Building and Rebuilding

School culture is the set of norms, values and beliefs, rituals and ceremonies, symbols and stories that make up the "persona" of the school.—Deal & Peterson, 1999

Walk into a school and pay attention to the climate. Does it feel welcoming? Do the students look and sound happy? Are the teachers engaged? Do you feel accepted? How the school feels, whether positive or negative, is a reflection of the climate. A positive school climate feels like the perfect warm, sunny day. A negative school climate feels like the cold, harsh winds of a Wisconsin winter storm. School climate affects relationships between the people working in the school and those experiencing the school.

School climate is the "feel," whereas the culture of a school is a sense of "how we do things around here." Culture reflects the values and norms of the school. But school culture is a somewhat slippery notion and may not be immediately felt or readily observed upon entering a school. However, culture can be seen in the school through the celebrations, rituals, and ceremonies valued by the school. The climate of a school can be changed quickly; however, changing the culture of a school is a slow and steady process that requires time, persistence, and leadership (Gruenert & Whitaker, 2015).

Being a literacy leader implies that the person possesses expertise in literacy. The literacy leader is someone teachers seek for sage advice on teaching and inspiring their students to become readers and writers. But what happens when the literacy leader is not the expert in literacy? What does it mean when the literacy leader has never even been a classroom teacher? What happens when the literacy leader is a school psychologist? What implications might this have on the established culture? What impact does it have on the climate?

Authors such as Routman (2014) specifically address the inadequacy of principals to lead schools in the area of literacy due to their lack of literacy knowledge. She is clear about the tensions that can arise from advocating for something where you lack expertise and understanding. This is a hard pill to swallow for a principal faced with improving student performance in the areas of reading and writing. This is exactly the situation Jason faced when he became principal.

CULTURE: THE CORNERSTONE TO LEARNING

When teachers are given the autonomy to make professional decisions, they can significantly impact the climate of a school. Teachers may feel invigorated, free from the prescribed curriculum, and free to direct their instruction to meet the needs of their students when given authority and support to make decisions for their students. Principals may also feel liberated when teachers are given autonomy. They are able to relax and trust that they have hired the right people to deliver the right instruction to the students.

A shift to greater teacher autonomy may be the shot in the arm a school needs to be revitalized, and it may be what is needed to improve the school climate. However, what happens when the climate changes as a result of increased teacher instructional autonomy and the culture remains the same? If the culture of the school is one that does not celebrate teacher growth, professionalism, and student success, then a shift in increased teacher autonomy may not be impactful. As literacy leaders, principals are in the position to ensure that they develop a positive school climate and culture that recognizes effort, celebrates teacher and student growth through clear expectations, and provides ongoing feedback.

The outside political pressures placed on schools to demonstrate student success based on measures of standardized tests have resulted in a steady attack on school cultures that value teacher autonomy designed to meet the needs of their students. One of the ways teacher autonomy has been undermined is by "creating a culture of dependency among teachers by overrating the expertise of published research and underrating the practical knowledge of teachers" (Fullan & Hargreaves, 1996, p. 24). The reliance on prepackaged curricula results in school cultures that celebrate teacher and student compliance rather than teacher and student risk-taking. As a result, teachers and students miss out on the powerful learning that teachers experience when they make decisions based on student needs.

What Tynisha, Margaret-Mary, and Jason have observed and experienced is this false kind of encouragement. In such instances, they have witnessed school principals fall into the trap, whether intentionally or unintentionally, of celebrating and rewarding compliance by conducting mandatory walk-throughs or completing evaluation procedures and then praising teachers who adhere to pacing schedules or post obligatory goal statements on classroom boards. Rather, what the authors hope to observe and experience are focused literacy lessons that include principals' reflective feedback regarding whether the students are learning authentic literacy skills and teachers are meeting individual literacy needs.

The cultures of many schools do not celebrate or ritualize teacher-to-student risk-taking, as evidenced by what is showcased. Grading systems result in one final grade. Student projects result in one final piece of work. Teacher evaluations focus on one to three observations over the course of any given year in which elementary teachers alone may teach nine hundred or more separate lessons.

If the culture of a school is to celebrate student learning and growth, then "we need to change our mindsets from merely getting curriculum covered to thinking more about how we learn, why we learn, and how we can have a larger impact on student learning" (DeWitt, 2017, p. 22). To create a strong school culture focused on student and teacher growth, the focus of celebrations and rituals should be on the process of learning and teaching, rather than on the end product of learning.

The cornerstone of an elementary school culture built on the process of student literacy learning is rich in expectations for high-quality instruction, student perseverance, teacher and student feedback, as well as student and teacher growth data. To set this as the cornerstone of learning can be more intensive and result in more work for the elementary school literacy leader. However, the work for the administrator is more significant, more enriching, and more purposeful because it sets the stage for teachers to be granted more autonomy while increasing student and teacher joy in the learning process. Requiring teachers to make informed professional decisions based on the needs of their students, not based on the pacing schedule of their district-provided curriculum, increases autonomy, and, in the process, increases joy and satisfaction.

The process of creating a strong culture must always be mindful "that our most well-intentioned commitments to effectiveness and improvements don't undermine what many teachers value most here—the time and opportunity to care for and teach their children" (Fullan & Hargreaves, 1996, p. 23). It is imperative that the principal, serving as the literacy leader, actively understands the importance of culture building. "Cultures do not lead; leaders lead. If the culture is leading, then the leader is only managing" (Gruenert & Whitaker, 2015, p. 31). How do we get to the important work of leading a culture?

ESTABLISHING A CULTURE OF TRUST

To be a literacy leader, one must believe that the classroom teachers—either inherited or hired—are doing what they believe to be in the best interests of their students, that they are the instructional leaders in their classrooms, and that they are committed to refining their craft. As literacy leaders, we must be willing to support teachers when changing their instructional practices. Teachers employ the best practices they know. If we ask them to change without support, their second instructional option may be worse (Whitaker, 2012).

If the student progress and achievement data do not support the effectiveness of the teacher's instructional practices, then it is up to the literacy leader to assist the teacher in developing his instructional capabilities. One way to begin this process is establishing a culture of trust between the teachers and the literacy leader. Just as a teacher can never give up on one of his students, a principal cannot give up on one of her teachers. A school culture will not be built and nurtured if there are conflicting commitments—one expectation for commitment to students and another opposing commitment to the students' teachers. When one outweighs the other, the school climate and culture unravel.

To build trust between the principal and the teachers is to be more present within their classrooms. It is imperative to let the teachers know that a principal is genuinely interested in their teaching and the learning of their students. If the principal does not take time to help teachers understand why he or she is visiting the classrooms, and if the principal does not clearly understand the objectives of visiting classrooms, the intent to build trust between the principal and the teachers can flounder or be damaged.

As Fullan and Hargreaves (1996) state, "Dropping in unannounced on a teacher's lesson, it is easy for the principal to take a dim view of the teacher found dictating notes or administering a spelling test, or assigning handwriting drills" (p. 33). When a principal sees these activities happening, rather than taking a dim view of the teacher's decision-making process, it is more productive and helpful to view the lesson from the teacher's perspective. Observations are frequent, and follow-up discussions or dialogues are customary. This is an expected practice on the part of the literacy leader. In chapter 8, the authors provide extensive insight into observations and feedback.

To understand the context and the purpose of the lesson, the teacher and principal must be able to dialogue about the instructional plan without fear of condemnation. Trust is built on dialogue. Foundational to this kind of practice is the notion that teachers are professionals who are trusted to make sound instructional decisions. A principal cannot assume the role of being a literacy leader and expect to understand every decision a teacher makes.

Teachers cannot be treated as mere technicians, designed to simply impart what a commercial product dictates. Teachers are not low-level employees, disallowed the autonomy to make decisions.

"Hired hands own nothing, are told what to do, and have little status in their enterprises. Teachers are often treated like hired hands. Not surprisingly they often act like hired hands" (Fullan & Hargreaves, 1996, pp. 35–36). A literacy leader cannot expect great things from teachers who function as hired hands. Teaching is an entirely human endeavor built on relationships, knowledge of sound instructional practices, and expertise of potential curriculum materials. When teachers are viewed as professionals and strong relationships are built, the climate and culture transforms, and the love of learning improves exponentially for students and teachers alike.

Visiting classrooms without leaving feedback for the teacher is simply a waste of time. The type and the form of feedback that is left can be tricky when trying to build trusting relationships. A teacher should not receive a visit and be left wondering the following:

- What was the purpose of the visit?
- Did I do well or not?
- What are the principal's thoughts about the visit?
- Will the visit be part of the annual evaluation process?

When there is teacher confusion about the purpose of the visit, student performance can be impacted. Fullan and Hargreaves (1996) found that when teachers are left with feedback that is not specific and leaves the teacher questioning the feedback, student gains in math and reading correlate negatively. Further, Rosenholtz (1989) posits that the absence of positive feedback may be the main culprit for the negative correlation. However, we contend that simply leaving a message of positive feedback or a checklist of required components can be transformative.

Teachers work hard. When a literacy leader acknowledges the teachers' hard work through honest and specific feedback, trust between the literacy leader and teachers will be cemented. The feedback must go beyond "good job." It should be intentional and connected to the reading beliefs of the school. Examples of sentence stems include:

- I noticed you allowed your students choice by . . .
- I noticed you connected with your students by . . .
- You engaged your students during read-aloud by . . .
- You coached your students by . . .

Using these sentence stems, or others similar to these, helps the literacy stay intentional in the feedback. This feedback is also specific. This is exactly what we expect our teachers to do for students. Why would we not expect the same level of intentional and specific feedback from a literacy leader to his or her teachers?

WE GET ALONG, HAVE FUN, AND LIKE EACH OTHER— THAT'S GOOD, RIGHT?

Everyone wants to have fun in life. Whether it is with family or friends, at work, or in the classroom, we all enjoy having fun. Students even learn more when the lessons they are presented with are engaging and relate to their lives. Daily decisions and resulting habits from those decisions have a huge impact on our levels of both happiness and success (Achor, 2011). School climates that are playful yet also serious, collaborative, and congenial make for great working environments. However, just because the teachers get along, have fun, and like each other does not translate to a climate that results in high learning expectations for students.

Sometimes being nice can get in the way of developing a culture that demands high expectations for teachers and students. "Being nice to each other is generally a good idea, but it can inhibit the practice of providing feedback in the form of criticism or even an alternative point of view" (Gruenert & Whitaker, 2015, p. 53). If the climate is one of congeniality between the teachers, it is fair to assume that the teachers may also be overly congenial to students and not offer constructive feedback that encourages the students to learn more and develop further than what they, themselves, expected.

The climate of a school must extend beyond simply being pleasant—that is a basic expectation of professionalism. School climate and resultant culture must be facilitated so that teachers and leaders engage in conversations that reflect opposing views, challenge established practices, and focus primarily on the needs of the students.

Unfortunately, literacy leaders often fail to move beyond a positive school climate to a culture of high expectations because "when we talk about school we seem to talk about adults a lot more than we talk about students" (DeWitt, 2017, p. 29). A literacy leader must understand the balance of facilitating a climate in which people enjoy their work, respect their colleagues, and enjoy coming to school. However, climate cannot come at the expense of student learning.

A strong school culture values the needs of its teachers and, at the same time, supports and maintains that the school structure exists for the students. To establish a congenial school climate that also has a strong school culture, "leaders must understand the uplifting effect on their people of open communication, keeping promises, recognizing great work, and work-life balance"

(Gostick & Elton, 2012, p. 57). If a literacy leader desires to make an impact on student learning, he or she must also remain committed to creating an environment in which teachers are respected as professionals within the school walls who also deserve to have a quality life outside of the classroom.

Creating a positive school climate is less challenging than reshaping a school's culture. "Whereas a change in climate can occur instantly, a change in culture is necessarily a slow evolution" (Gruenert & Whitaker, 2015, p. 15). The challenge for a literacy leader is to recognize the process of moving from a positive school climate to an impactful school culture that is not only positive but also challenging and inquisitive and includes open communication.

Many literacy leaders spend time trying to influence individuals to change, hoping that once they have convinced individuals to make changes, a school culture will be transformed. This tactic is misguided. Gostick and Elton (2012), remind us that "it may take a long time for a manager to influence a person, but once a collective culture is established it can change people in a hurry. Culture can influence perspectives, expectations, belief systems, and even the biology of their members" (pp. 40–41). Focusing on creating a school culture grounded in teacher and student autonomy, joy, choice, and informed decision-making can result in a paradigm shift that runs deeper than changing one teacher or student at a time.

Open communication between the literacy leader and those who may not hold the title as principal is critical in advancing a positive school climate and culture. "Heaven knows how much value is squandered by leaders who do not spend time engaging their people—those who don't recognize their dependence on their subordinates" (Gostick & Elton, 2012, p. 52). One way to avoid squandering the value of teachers within the school is to genuinely listen.

JASON'S STORY: WHEN THERE IS A CULTURE CLASH

The positive climate in the building had been well-established by the previous administration. People liked each other and got along. The previous administration had been there for over a decade. In addition, the building represents the research regarding gender demographics in most elementary schools. The principal and associate principal were White women and had spent time as elementary teachers. Jason had not.

Jason introduced a little more fun into the building and was able to maintain the family atmosphere of the building. There was an existing culture. Because of that culture, Jason's efforts were received well by the staff and the students. The belief that teachers should enjoy autonomy in their teaching and students should experience joy in their learning was also received well.

Parents, teachers, support staff, and students expressed a love for the school and the good "feel" of the building. However, the good feel of the building only went so far. The instructional message of high standards for teaching and learning was being lost in the desire to experience autonomy, joy, and fun. From Jason's perspective as the literacy leader, teachers were enjoying teaching, students were enjoying learning, and everyone was happy. It seemed that a former school psychologist who had never been in the classroom could be a literacy leader. But then it happened.

The focus on teacher autonomy, student choice, and joy were being challenged by an adoption of a new literacy resource. This placed Jason in conflict with the district's director of curriculum and his own literacy coach. The ensuing months were rife with intense conversations, debate, and in some cases, direct attempts to undermine the resource-adoption process.

As the instructional leader of the building, Jason maintained his belief that teacher-created materials were far superior to anything that could be purchased from a publishing company. Ultimately, his belief that he knew better damaged the trust he had established with his literacy coach. Jason was never an elementary teacher, he was not a reading specialist, and that was made very clear to him. The conflict was beginning to slowly erode the climate that had been built and was creating a culture in which the principal was the only voice that mattered when making instructional decisions. Finally, after increasing tensions, Jason invited his literacy coach to lunch so they could discuss the direction of the purchase and what would be best for the teachers and students of the school.

During the lunch conversation, Jason came to realize that he could continue to be the leader of the building—the instructional leader, the literacy leader. He would be able to facilitate the continued creation of the climate and culture and the vision for instruction, but he had to realize he did not have the expertise to understand all the complexities of literacy. This was the role of the literacy coach. He had to be the literacy leader who understood his limits, and in the same way, he had to humble himself so others could lead with his support. Most importantly, he had to listen.

A LESSON LEARNED

To be a literacy leader, one has to be vulnerable. A literacy leader has to know his role, has to know the limits of his expertise, and has to trust the expertise among the faculty in the building. The lunch meeting that was an open exchange of ideas and built on trusting relationships resulted in an epiphany of sorts for Jason.

Prior to the meeting, he had been a literacy leader who believed he had to maintain to the appearance that he was an expert in literacy. After the meeting, he continued to be a literacy leader, but he began to rely on the expertise of others to collaboratively assist him in establishing the vision and the culture of literacy for the school. His literacy coach taught him a valuable lesson that he was open to receiving and internalizing.

A strong climate and culture around literacy can suffer setbacks and requires continual rebuilding. The rebuilding can only occur when the leader of the building is willing to listen and trust his subordinates. Again, the authors of this text turn to Gostick and Elton (2012) in explaining, "In addition, a good portion of an enabling (support) leader's time is spent helping his or her people steer their way through choppy waters—not solving employee problems per se, but providing the communication employees need to make wise decisions in a changing environment, as well as offering the tools, resources, and clear expectations to help employees move forward successfully" (p. 53).

This statement applies to both the subordinates and the leader. To have a trusting culture and climate, literacy leaders must recognize that they also require support and that those they supervise can assist them in steering their way through the choppy waters of literacy leadership. Literacy leaders like Jason must be open to being lifelong learners themselves.

This chapter discusses culture and climate. Both of these, if not positive, can have a detrimental ripple effect on the many stakeholders who are invested in the success of the school. Maintaining culture and addressing breeches when they occur is not an easy task; it's daunting, draining, and demanding. It is necessary for the instructional leader of the building.

The authors have heard many times, as it relates to classroom culture, that if you don't set the expectations in the classroom, someone will. This is true for the culture of a school as well. If the principal as the literacy leader does not set the culture, then someone will. Chapter 7 makes a shift from culture and climate to professional development and the role of professional development communities.

REFLECTION QUESTIONS

- How would you describe the climate of your building?
- How would you describe the culture of your building?
- How would your instructional staff describe the culture and climate of your building?
- How would you respond if they do not align?
- What internal and/or external factors may be in conflict with what you want to be true for the literacy culture in your building?

- How will you address the conflict while maintaining a positive building culture?

REFERENCES

Achor, S. (2011). *The happiness advantage: The seven principles that fuel success and performance at work.* London, UK: Virgin.

Deal, T. E., & Peterson, K. D. (1999). *Shaping school culture: The heart of leadership.* Hoboken, NJ: John Wiley & Sons.

DeWitt, P. (2017). *Collaborative leadership: Six influences that matter most.* Thousand Oaks, CA: Corwin.

Fullan, M., & Hargreaves, A. (1996). *What's worth fighting for in your school?* New York, NY: Teachers College Press.

Gostick, A., & Elton, C. (2012). *All in: How the best managers create a culture of belief and drive big results.* New York, NY: Free Press.

Gruenert, S., & Whitaker, T. (2015). *School culture rewired: How to define, assess, and transform it.* Alexandria, VA: ASCD.

Routman, R. (2014). *Read, write, lead: Breakthrough strategies for schoolwide literacy success.* Alexandria, VA: ASCD.

Rosenholtz, S. J. (1989). Workplace conditions that affect teacher quality and commitment: Implications for teacher induction programs. *Elementary School Journal, 89*(4), 421–439.

Whitaker, T. (2012). *What great principals do differently: Eighteen things that matter most* (2nd ed.). New York, NY: Routledge.

Chapter Seven

From "One-Size-Fits-All" Professional Development to Professional Development Communities

I hope when I die, it's during a school professional development session. The transition will be slight.—Anonymous Teacher

When Jason was a practicing school psychologist, one of the most frustrating experiences was attending professional development days. Please note, Jason was a school psychologist for many years and never a classroom teacher. Often the professional development offered by the school district was a "one-size-fits-all" model. The content was classroom-teacher-specific, which makes sense, as the majority of the participants were classroom teachers.

Teacher-specific professional development seemed strange, as it was expected that a school psychologist, an art teacher, a physical education teacher, or a speech and language therapist would find value in attending professional development specifically designed to increase the efficacy of classroom teachers' ability to teach literacy. Yet Jason, who may be viewed in a way similar to many specialists, spent a day with great teachers, scratching his head and asking himself: *Why am I here? How is this relevant to my work?*

Tynisha, however, as a classroom teacher who was responsible for teaching all fourth grade literacy one year, had a very different experience. She would find herself in professional development held by a presenter who had not been in the classroom for a long time, did not know her students, but was considered a national expert. Tynisha is not opposed to national experts, but she vividly remembers spending three days learning a specific literacy approach curriculum that was meant to stand alone. This new approach, while intended to stand alone, was also designed specifically to increase test scores.

The curriculum development officers at the district level required the new curriculum to be used in conjunction with the core reading program, for which Tynisha attended several professional development sessions the previous year. In addition, the district required all schools to follow the 11 x 17 neon-pink-covered scope and sequence manual for literacy. Yes, there was a professional development day specifically designed for how to read the grade-level-specific literacy scope and sequence. The result of the varied professional development sessions and time away from classroom instruction was that Tynisha left too many professional developments feeling professionally devalued.

Margaret-Mary taught high school English and middle-level language arts and was a Title I pull-out literacy specialist for a total of fifteen years in public school classrooms. Margaret-Mary recalls a mix of professional development sessions. In her high school teaching, all faculty professional development was geared toward common issues, and discipline-specific professional development occurred, for instance, with all the English teachers. In middle school, she recalls her professional development sessions as Jason did. She endured years of discussions about scheduling (she had no input) or how to best provide access to computer labs. Very little of what was discussed pertained to her.

As an elementary literacy specialist, she experienced yet another iteration of professional development. She vividly remembers one principal who delivered professional development that pertained to all, such as classroom management, but who also asked faculty to lead sessions wherein expertise and ideas were shared. This principal epitomized shared leadership in that she first asked teachers what they needed; then she facilitated sessions that were germane to individual faculty.

In other words, faculty had choice. This same principal also scheduled professional development for all faculty around daily writing in all subjects, increasing reading time, and once, how different disciplines could work together and create text sets around themes (topics) taught in English language arts, math, social studies, and science. This principal both knew her faculty and trusted their expertise.

PROFESSIONAL DEVELOPMENT QUALITY

Based on the work of Guskey (1986), professional development has the distinct potential to impact the process of instructional change. Guskey (2000) promotes active evaluation of professional development as a part of what schools do in terms of improving instruction as a means of impacting student outcomes. His model of evaluating professional development includes five phases of evaluation:

1. participants' response to the process;
2. participants' knowledge acquisition;
3. organizational support for change;
4. participants' utilization and implementation of the knowledge and skills gained; and
5. the discernable impact of the professional development process on student outcomes.

Teachers consider professional development applicable when it directly addresses their specific needs and concerns (Guskey, 1995).

Research findings from the field of educational leadership strongly suggest that leadership in a school setting influences professional learning through professional development. Guskey's model (1995, 2000) assumes *response* to the professional development process as well as presuming participants will acquire knowledge and that the organization (school or district) provides support for change. Furthermore, Guskey's (1995, 2000) model also suggests that the knowledge and skill sets acquired by participants, specifically the influences and impact of the professional development process, in turn, will influence and impact student outcomes.

Aligned with Guskey's model of professional development, DuFour's model (2007, 2011) of professional development recommends the establishment of learning communities, a concept and configuration that includes high levels of engagement and collaboration. Fullan (1995) strongly suggests that professional learning models must include reflection about the professional development process and the creation of collaborative learning spaces. Job-embedded professional development engages teachers in learning through their daily activities, roles, and responsibilities and is embedded within teaching as opposed to being separate from teachers' everyday issues and concerns.

Thus, the research on professional development from the last several decades recommends teachers working collaboratively in job-embedded teams as a viable form of professional development. However, it is also clear from the research that making time for sustained job-embedded professional development is a vital consideration.

The notion of making time extends beyond the obligatory monthly or even weekly professional development opportunities and can include release time to observe other teachers or attend professional meetings, symposiums, and conferences; restructured or rescheduled time within a day such as when cocurricular instruction is scheduled or when vertical teaming can occur; common planning time such as grade-level time; and purchased time like weekends or breaks when teachers can plan while being paid (Darling-Hammond, 2000; Guskey, 1999).

A lack of adequate time built into a school's calendar and schedule is a major barrier to effective job-embedded professional development. It is a literacy leader's responsibility to plan time for professional development. Hirsch and Hord (2012) directly focus on the role of leaders in creating the optimum conditions for high-quality professional learning:

> Leaders are responsible for communicating the importance of professional learning and advocating for it for all educators. They engage with stakeholders at all levels within and outside the organization to discuss the importance of investing in professional learning and to describe the connection between professional learning and the system's goals for staff and students. (pp. 47–48)

CHOICE AS A PART OF PROFESSIONAL DEVELOPMENT

In chapter 6, the authors discussed the importance of establishing trust as a critical component in creating a school climate and culture. Trust is equally important when discussing professional development options for teachers. The authors agree that certain professional development topics are required for all teachers regardless of their position. Topics such as mandatory reporting of potential child abuse, active shooter drills (an unfortunate reality), mandates that trickle down from central office, and trauma sensitivity may be a few examples.

Research suggests that too much choice can result in a lack of focus for teachers: "Their physical stamina, ability to perform numerical calculations, persistence in the face of failure, and overall focus can drop dramatically" (Achor, 2010, p. 166). Maybe that's why school administrators have presented professional development as limited choice: to protect the stamina of their teachers. The authors don't think so. Jason, Margaret-Mary, and Tynisha believe school administrators do this to manage accountability and to provide uniformity in instruction. This is counterintuitive to the position that teachers should be attending to the individual needs of their students through differentiated instruction practices.

A literacy leader expects teachers to recognize the unique learning needs of their students and requires teachers to differentiate and, in some cases, personalize their instruction. If this is the case, then why do we expect all teachers to experience the same professional development? Failing to recognize the individual learning needs of teachers minimizes them as individuals and professionals.

The research clearly suggests that the elementary school's literacy leader has ultimate responsibility to create, facilitate, and support professional development opportunities. However, choice is somewhat ambiguous. Achor

(2010) argues that too much choice can be counterproductive. Pink (2009) maintains that without choice, employees become disenfranchised and lose their creativity and desire to complete their jobs. For literacy leaders, it is imperative to have a balance between the "one-size-fits-all" professional development and the need for choice in selecting professional development opportunities.

Trusting teachers to participate in continued professional development is paramount to the literacy leader's role. When we don't trust that our teachers will continue to develop professionally, we minimize them as professionals. Teachers also have the responsibility to seek out new learning opportunities and to employ recommended practices.

Most people would not choose a doctor to perform surgery on them or their loved one if the doctor was using the same surgical procedures he or she learned in 1982. Just like doctors, teachers cannot rely on the instructional materials and pedagogy from 1982. To demonstrate the value of teachers as professionals and the role of professional development, teachers should be able to select what is best for their own professional growth.

As authors who have experienced professional development, delivered professional development, and supported teachers, Tynisha, Margaret-Mary, and Jason acknowledge that not all professional development is created equal. In their roles of supporting teachers, there are times where each of them had to be more prescriptive and require teachers to attend specific types of professional development.

While a teacher knows what she needs professionally, an attentive literacy leader can augment what a teacher needs professionally. This knowledge is only a result of strong relationships and trust. An effective leader can also identify teachers who have the capacity to provide professional development for other teachers in the building. What the authors argue is that not all professional development must come from a national expert. In fact, schools are full of experts. But how do you offer choice?

FROM PROFESSIONAL LEARNING COMMUNITIES TO PROFESSIONAL DEVELOPMENT COMMUNITIES

To tap the experts in his building, Jason hosted a planning day with his teacher-leaders in the spring of 2013. During the day, the leaders reviewed student data. Through the review, the teacher-leaders identified twelve areas in which they felt the staff could benefit from professional development. Some of the topics included:

- guided reading;
- the components of balanced literacy;

- project-based learning;
- incorporating play into the kindergarten curriculum;
- classroom management and classroom culture;
- self-selected book studies;
- lines of difference and other issues of diversity; and
- trauma-sensitive schools.

The only condition the teacher-leaders had was that the topics had to connect to the established reading beliefs:

- Student choice and easy access to books influence motivation and achievement.
- Time should be made for read-alouds and independent reading on a regular basis.
- Positive relationships and connections can be built through reading.

The connection to the reading beliefs was critical to embed the beliefs as part of the school culture when it came to literacy. The teaching staff had unanimously selected these as the beliefs of the school. Ignoring them would have rendered them unimportant to the culture.

The teacher leaders decided to seek out experts in the building to facilitate the sessions. If experts could not be found, then outside experts were contracted to deliver the professional development. Once the facilitators had been secured, the rest of the teaching staff was given the opportunity to choose their top three choices for professional development. The scheduled professional development communities would be held on Wednesdays prior to the start of the instructional day. The communities met twice a month. It was the expectation that they would record their learning and share it with the other communities so everyone would have exposure to the learning.

The response was overwhelmingly positive. Teachers appreciated having choice. Additionally, they reported feeling satisfied that they were treated as professionals when directing their own learning. Some changes did need to be made during the course of the school year. In spite of having a great deal of choice, there were a few members of the staff who felt their learning needs were not being met. They proposed new learning opportunities and were allowed to pursue those interests. The opportunity for choice in learning reenergized the professional development activities.

WHAT IS A PROFESSIONAL DEVELOPMENT COMMUNITY?

DuFour is often credited as the creator of the professional learning community (PLC) framework, which has transformed instruction, teacher collaboration, and student achievement (DuFour & Eaker, 1998). Other researchers have also investigated and reported on the PLC model (Cranston, 2009; Harris & Jones, 2010; Maloney & Konza, 2011; Olivier, 2001) What makes the professional development community (PDC) inherently different from the PLC is that it focuses on the teacher's individual learning through exploration, collaboration, and discussion (DuFour, 2004). The PDC serves two purposes: (1) to differentiate/personalize teacher learning opportunities and (2) to improve communication and collaboration between grade levels and academic disciplines.

There is power in the discussion that happens in a PDC when a first grade teacher, a special education teacher, a school psychologist, an art teacher, and the library media specialist discuss instructional practices within the scope of the schoolwide reading beliefs. An unintended consequence of the discussions is that the instructional staff form relationships, which leads to teachers visiting other teachers' classrooms to observe and learn. Teachers find themselves engaging in discussions about student learning, pedagogy, and their overall passion for teaching—the exact conversations that are not regularly occurring in "one-size-fits-all" professional development sessions.

The PDC framework served to revitalize veteran teachers who had grown tired of "one-size-fits-all" professional development sessions. As one teacher whom Jason supervises shared, "The excitement, the discussion, and freedom to discuss teaching as our craft was exhilarating. It was fun to share my expertise and learn from the new teachers. It made me excited to teach again." It also made them feel like professionals again. They were trusted to have professional discussions without being monitored by administration. It was a free exchange of ideas—the same free exchange we want to see from students when discussing the book they just read or the piece of writing they completed.

WHERE DO PROFESSIONAL DEVELOPMENT COMMUNITIES FIT?

For a literacy leader who values the concept of professional development communities, the question is not *Where do they fit?* but *How can you afford not to make them fit?* A literacy leader is in charge of creating a climate and culture that focuses on a commitment to literacy. With leadership, teachers within a school community can acquire deep literacy content knowledge, address persistent issues, use appropriate literacy pedagogical practices strategically, and create their own solutions in the best interest of their students. Professional development is the key to maintaining a commitment to literacy. There is time within every school schedule, as the research suggests (Darling-Hammond, 2000; Guskey, 1999). It may be hidden, but the time is there and can be found.

Jason found the time by listening to teacher-leaders within his faculty. They requested that the forty-five minutes of planning time before school be used on Wednesday mornings twice a month. One of the remaining Wednesdays was reserved for a faculty meeting. The other remaining Wednesday was for planning or other meetings. The two Wednesday mornings for PDC were nonnegotiable.

Jason also offered that Friday mornings before school would be "off limits" for scheduled meetings. This time was reserved for team or individual planning. The remaining mornings of the week would be used for any other types of meetings. Through this schedule, there were ninety minutes per month dedicated to teacher-directed, literacy-specific professional development. The impact was significant.

As one teacher noted,

> I have not had discussions about reading or writing with my team like this for years. We aren't in the same PDC and we can't wait to meet to discuss what the other PDCs talked about. I feel that I am sharing and learning more than I ever had.

Another teacher mentioned that for the first time in her twenty-plus years of education, she felt like she had been valued as a professional because she was trusted to find her learning based on what she knew was in the best interest of her kids. That same teacher also shared she had been considering retirement but now thought she may "stick around awhile" to see "how this all plays out."

Trusting teachers to choose their learning based on their needs made them feel like professionals. When teachers feel like professionals, they can focus on the important job of instilling the joy of learning in their students. Carving time out of a schedule took effort, but collaboratively, Jason and the teachers with whom he worked found a solution that worked. Because teachers created a solution and time for literacy discussions, they possessed ownership over the solution and the process.

INVESTING IN TEACHERS

Where to spend limited school funds is a challenging issue for literacy leaders. Allocating funds for instructional materials and resources can be an appealing and quick fix when schools are struggling to help students improve their literacy skills. Purchasing materials means all teachers will be using the same items, teaching the same scope and sequence, having common language when instructing their students, and using materials backed by research. But materials alone don't equate to improved student learning. Investing in teachers and developing their skills through professional development leads to a professionally trained staff who has the innate tools to address the individual learning needs of its students.

Jason's next step in continuing PDCs was to provide teachers the opportunity to connect with educators outside of their building and their district. Jason did this by reallocating his budget so teachers could attend regional, state, and national conferences focused on literacy. The first group to be taken to a national conference were members of the literacy leadership team. While this may seem obvious, the shift in sending teachers to national conferences did not come without challenges.

The challenge can be summed up in one word: fairness. School budgets continued to shrink. A shrinking budget did not allow for all teachers to attend a conference. Jason had to be strategic and select teachers who served on the literacy leadership team, had a background in literacy, or needed the most professional development in literacy. Additionally, the teachers selected had to accept the responsibility of returning and sharing their learning with colleagues. Not surprisingly, the teachers understood this process and agreed to it. Teachers felt valued as professionals, and they trusted that the selection process was done in the best interests of the teaching staff and, most importantly, with the students in mind.

Moving toward PDCs and strategic, differentiated, and personalized learning for teachers means understanding the learning needs of teachers. A principal who is a literacy leader must understand where his or her teachers are in their ability to deliver literacy instruction. Often in schools, veteran teachers are left alone. They are trusted to deliver content and have demonstrated through evaluations that they have the ability to do so effectively. It is the novice teachers who get the most attention and support. After the novice teachers have demonstrated proficiency, they enter the pool and are seemingly left alone to instruct. Jason had heard this from other principals: "I don't feel the need to visit my good teachers. They are doing their job. It is my job to leave them alone and let them do it."

Jason was left with the following question: *Is this what we would expect from a teacher who has a high-achieving student—let them alone to do their own thing and not provide any feedback in order to advance their learning further?* Additionally, if veteran teachers are left alone and the classrooms that are visited are only the ones of new teachers, then is it not implied that a classroom visit or invitation to participate in professional development is not about growth but deficiency?

The challenge of including free choice in the professional development community model is providing guided choice for teachers who may need extra support. Jason overcame this by being visible in classrooms, speaking his truth, and having the courage to hold brutally honest discussions that focused on teacher growth rather than deficiency. He reasoned that as he would not accept a heart surgeon operating on his kids using the same methods for twenty years, he could not accept that from his teachers.

Regardless of how "good" teachers were or how much experience they had, Jason expected that the reading beliefs of choice, time, and relationships would be adhered to through professional development. And you know what? The teachers who worked with Jason did it because they wanted what was best for their students and were willing to do whatever it took to get it done.

THE CONSEQUENCE OF PDCS

The positive consequence of PDCs was the number of teachers who sought their own professional development opportunities through local, state, and national organizations in Jason's school. Teachers began connecting with other teachers by joining the Wisconsin Reading Association, International Literacy Association, and the Association of Curriculum Supervision and Development, among others. Additionally, there was an increase in the number of requests for professional books for grassroots book discussions within the building. The opportunity to discuss and improve their skills as teachers motivated faculty to find time to become active professionals who discuss their craft regularly.

Chapter 7 takes a deep dive in creating a culture where professional development is valued, nonpunitive, and differentiated. The authors recognize that teachers need different types of development based on what they are teaching, who they teach, and what they need to refine their craft. Professional development needs shift over time and are impacted by outside forces and by existing and new faculty members. The authors argue for a differentiated approach to professional development; however, they recognize that there are also common development opportunities that everyone must attend.

Ultimately, it is up to the literacy leader to assist with creating the culture to ensure that professional development highlights and prioritizes what is valuable for all teachers to be the best literacy teachers. Chapter 8 will provide insight into the journey of the literacy leader as evaluator and assessor. These responsibilities can be challenging; however, the authors have found evaluation and assessment to be necessary to ensure a culture where literacy beliefs are actualized.

REFLECTION QUESTIONS

- What were the past instructional foci of literacy instruction in your school and district?

- How can professional learning about literacy among school faculty be facilitated?
- How would you differentiate professional development in your building?
- In what types of development would you want your teachers to participate?
- How can you reallocate time or create time for teacher-led professional development?
- Who are the teachers and other instructional staff you could leverage to develop professional opportunities?
- How can faculty working together increase and improve literacy instruction in order to produce progressively sophisticated student writers?

REFERENCES

Achor, S. (2010). *The happiness advantage: The seven principles of positive psychology that fuel performance and success at work.* New York, NY: Crown Business.

Cranston, J. (2009). Holding the reins of the professional learning community: Eight themes from research on principals' perceptions of professional learning communities. *Canadian Journal of Educational Administration and Policy, 90,* 1–22.

Darling-Hammond, L. (2000). Teacher quality and student achievement. *Education Policy Analysis Archives, 8,* 1. Retrieved from http://epaa.asu.edu/ojs/article/view/392/515

DuFour, R. (2004). What is a "professional learning community"? *Educational Leadership, 61*(8), 6–11.

DuFour, R. (2007). Professional learning communities: A bandwagon, an idea worth considering, or our best hope for high levels of learning? *Middle School Journal, 39*(1), 4–8.

DuFour, R. (2011). Work together: But only if you want to. *Phi Delta Kappan, 92*(5), 57–61.

DuFour, R., & Eaker, R. (1998). *Professional learning communities at work: Best practices for enhancing student achievement.* Bloomington, IN: Solution Tree.

Fullan, M. G. (1995). The limits and the potential of professional development. In T. Guskey and M. Huberman (Eds.), *Professional development in education: New paradigms and practices* (pp. 253–267). New York, NY: Teachers College Press.

Guskey, T. R. (1986). Staff development and the process of teacher change. *Educational Researcher, 15*(5), 5–12.

Guskey, T. R. (1995). Professional development in education: In search of the optimal mix. In T. Guskey & M. Huberman (Eds.), *Professional development in education: New paradigms and practices* (pp. 114–131). New York, NY: Teachers College Press.

Guskey, T. R. (1999, Spring). Apply time with wisdom. *Journal of Staff Development, 20*(2), 10–15.

Guskey, T. R. (2000). *Evaluating professional development.* Thousand Oaks, CA: Corwin Press.

Harris, A., & Jones, M. (2010). Professional learning communities and system improvement. *Improving Schools, 13*(2), 172–181.

Hirsch, S., & Hord, S. (2012). *A playbook for professional learning: Putting the standards into action.* Oxford, OH: Learning Forward.

Maloney, C., & Konza, D. M. (2011). A case study of teachers' professional learning: Becoming a community of professional learning or not? *Issues in Educational Research, 21*(1), 75–87.

Olivier, D. F. (2001). *Teacher personal and school culture characteristics in effective schools: Toward a model of a professional learning community.* An unpublished doctoral dissertation. Baton Rouge, LA: Louisiana State University.

Pink, D. (2009). *Drive: The surprising truth about what motivates us.* New York, NY: Riverhead Books.

Chapter Eight

Speaking Your Truth through Observing Literacy Teaching and Learning

And the truth shall set you free.—John 8:32 (KJV)

For literacy leaders, it's problematic to make recommendations and not be able to cogently discuss them or comment on them with some degree of expertise. A literacy leader cannot "talk the talk without walking the walk." Teachers are expected to provide feedback to their students frequently, with a purpose, and timely. As literacy leaders, we have the responsibility to provide the same level of feedback to our teachers. The feedback of the literacy leader must be frequent, purposeful, specific, and timely. This is a nonnegotiable practice of a literacy leader.

GETTING INTO CLASSROOMS: YOU HAVE TO DO IT

There are a multitude of responsibilities facing the building principal as the administrator and even more so as the literacy leader. As we have discussed in previous chapters, the very nature of a literacy leader's responsibilities is daunting. A literacy leader manages and supervises (Leithwood, Louis, Anderson, & Wahlstrom, 2004). This individual is responsible for school safety, student discipline, staffing, parent phone calls, budget, delivery of content, adherence to curriculum, bussing, making sure lunch is served . . . well, the list goes on and on. In the authors' experiences, with a high degree of frequency, an elementary literacy leader operates alone—with faculty of course—but without the additional support of assistant principals commonly found in secondary schools.

A literacy leader also sets the tone for both development and enactment of a school's literacy vision and mission (Hallinger & Heck, 2002). He assumes instructional leadership responsibilities (Bickmore & Sulentic Dowell, 2011; Hallinger, 2003, 2011; Hallinger & Murphy, 1985; Zepeda, 2007) and, specific to this text, guides and supports actual literacy leadership (Booth & Rowsell, 2007; Hoewing & Sulentic Dowell, 2010; Sulentic Dowell, 2012; Sulentic Dowell, Hoewing, & Bickmore, 2012). All of the tasks listed reflect the managerial responsibilities of the principal, as described previously in chapter 1.

In educational leadership literature, few studies reflect the leadership responsibilities of the principal who also serves as literacy leader. A principal who intends to be the literacy leader cannot lead from her office, but must lead from the front line. That means leadership begins and ends in the classroom. The authors of this text refer to this as the "point-of-service" delivery. Other than maintaining the safety of the school, there is nothing more important than observing teachers and student learning. A literacy leader must have a regular presence in all classrooms. This is not, however, the presence of the disciplinarian or as just the evaluator of instruction.

Getting into classrooms means getting rid of the excuses of why it can't be done. So, stop making excuses and do it. Instruction at the elementary level should have a sharp focus on the foundational skills of literacy. A literacy leader cannot ascertain if literacy instruction is effective without knowing and understanding what happens in classrooms surrounding literacy teaching and learning. Frequent classroom visits allow a literacy leader to check the pulse of a classroom (indicative of climate) and to determine if literacy is being taught and learned as faculty aspire to in their belief statements about literacy, and any subsequent mission and vision statements about literacy (which reflect culture).

Jason wrestled with this very issue as he was beginning to get into classrooms as a novice literacy leader. He was both clear about and comfortable with management issues and to some extent instructional supervision; however, he didn't quite grasp the importance of being seen in classrooms as a part of the school's literacy culture. Jason generated all kinds of excuses as to why he couldn't make regular, frequent classroom visits and observations work. He recalls, "There are just too many classrooms," or "How can I be expected to observe the teaching of fifty-plus teachers each week?" and "If I start doing regular walk-throughs, the teachers think I'm out to get them. I trust them, so why do I need to observe them?" and maybe the biggest concern: "I've never been a classroom teacher, so how can I give feedback on literacy if I've never taught it?"

Every argument Jason made was valid. Each excuse was a potential hurdle that needed to be addressed. The truth, however, is that each one was also a lousy excuse! Jason was creating excuses intended to avoid the hard work of being a literacy leader. This became apparent at a conference on teacher observation and evaluation, and his lack of awareness hit Jason hard. Jason attended the Association of School Administrators Conference in the spring semester of 2016, feeling like he was managing his school campus and that he was assuming leadership responsibilities well.

At the conference, Jason learned the following information that rocked his world: *Elementary teachers deliver over nine hundred lessons each school year* (Weston, 2014). If a teacher is only formally evaluated once every three years, and during their evaluation year they are only observed three times, it does not provide a good indication of the teacher's skills. That means over the course of three years a teacher will provide approximately 2,700 lessons. If only three lessons are observed over the span of three years, that means the principal makes a judgment on the teacher's performance based on 0.11 percent of her lessons. If the teacher provides three outstanding lessons during observations, typically scheduled in advance, she is deemed to be effective. In fact, she could be struggling daily. The inverse could also be true. So, advises Jason, get out of the office. All the other stuff can wait.

Literacy leaders will find no greater joy in their days than observing the greatest of their teachers and the learning their students experience. Walk-throughs became so important to Jason that when he couldn't visit classrooms, the absence of doing so gave him an unsettling feeling. When this happened, his administrative assistant, Lynne, would come into his office, give him a legal pad, and tell him what he was failing to recognize himself: "Go observe classrooms because you are a grumpy pain-in-the-butt today." Jason maintains that walk-throughs make everyone happier.

PRIORITIZING OBSERVATIONS AND WALK-THROUGHS

A literacy leader who prioritizes visiting and observing classrooms regularly must have a plan. When Jason initially started, he did not have a plan. He visited classrooms when he could. Some days he would visit three or four classrooms. Other days he would visit as many as seven. In fact, some days, he didn't see any instruction. There was no focus to the visits. He would visit classrooms, observe, talk to students, and leave. He felt good that he had visited a classroom, made himself visible, and showed support for his teachers. From Jason's point of view, he was on the right path, and he was giddy about that.

Teachers on the receiving end felt differently. Jason exited each room feeling excited. He was convinced he was making a difference. Instead, his teachers were left feeling confused. When Jason visited classrooms, there was no intentionality, no feedback, and no consistent plan for the classroom walk-throughs. Jason was missing the key ingredients to being a literacy leader committed to supporting teachers. But Jason needed his faculty to tell him this, as he failed to recognize it himself.

One teacher shared with Jason, "I'm glad you visit, but what are you looking for? You come in and leave. Am I doing okay, or is there a problem?" This sentiment was shared by many of the teachers. Some would stop in his office after the walk-through to find out what his impressions were of their teaching, but many did not. The other issue that arose was Jason fell into an unintentional pattern. He only visited certain teachers and at certain times. His walk-throughs lacked intentionality and were not a priority, so he assumed a "catch as catch can" attitude. He was not witnessing varied lessons or observing all of the school's teachers.

How could he be a literacy leader if he wasn't seeing everything and everyone? Acknowledging this was something he had to face. Jason had to confront his fears as a developing literacy leader. He had to make walk-throughs an intentional, daily priority. He also had to figure out what to look for and how to connect everything back to the reading beliefs he had established at the beginning of the year:

- choice;
- time; and
- relationships.

WHAT TO LOOK FOR

At the outset, Jason did not know what specific features of literacy instruction he should be looking for during walk-throughs. He knew how to look for classroom management and student engagement, but literacy practices were different. If he was going to do this, he needed help, and recognizing he needed guidance was a first step in Jason's solution. He reached out to the district curriculum director, his associate principal, a literacy coach, and Tynisha.

Tynisha was the ideal individual to add to Jason's accountability and support system because she supported him in his licensure-renewal process. Part of his process was to earn six graduate credits. He took two courses with Tynisha, and one was specifically focused on literacy leadership. It was in this course that Jason embraced his role as literacy leader.

Simply put, Jason had to acknowledge his weakness. For a leader, this is humbling and frightening, and it is a vulnerable position to find oneself. Jason ultimately knew if he wanted his teachers to experience autonomy and joy in their teaching and his students to experience joy in their learning, then his feelings could not matter. He put his ego aside and sought what he then recognized he needed to be an effective literacy leader.

The first step was to identify what was important to see during a walk-through. Jason's district and school follow a balanced literacy approach to instruction. During a walk-through, Jason had to observe the elements of balanced literacy:

- read-aloud;
- guided reading;
- shared reading;
- interactive writing;
- shared writing; and
- word study.

Working together as a group, they decided that classroom management techniques needed to be observed and levels of student engagement needed to be assessed. Additionally, the focus was going to be on teacher and student interaction. Other walk-through trainings Jason had attended focused on anchor charts and learning targets being on display as well as classroom layout. Jason and his colleagues agreed these were not going to be elements that needed to be commented on during the walk-through.

The "look for" list of student engagement, evidence of real reading and writing (not activities *about* reading and writing), and components of balanced literacy were established. Jason then felt confident about his task as an observer within a literacy framework. It was time to practice.

Along with the director of curriculum, his associate principal, other principals, and the literacy coach, Jason observed teachers and students together. After the walk-throughs, they would share their impressions and what type of feedback they would leave for the teacher. It was exciting for Jason to be collaborative, and he reveled in having rich discussions about instruction and student learning. However, something was still missing. The connection to the reading beliefs his faculty created was absent.

HOW BELIEFS INFORM THE WALK-THROUGH

Jason devoted a great deal of time to encouraging teachers to use the reading beliefs of choice, time, and relationships as a framework for making curricular and instructional decisions. Tynisha pointed out during a reflective conversation that the beliefs were not serving as the foundation for the intentional classroom walk-throughs. It was important to consider the components of balanced literacy, classroom management, and student engagement. If the reading beliefs were to be part of the cultural fabric of the school, then they had to be specifically observed instructionally. Tynisha believed if Jason did not intentionally look for evidence of the beliefs, he would not achieve his goal of creating autonomy and joy for his teachers and students.

To achieve this, Tynisha and Jason crafted and developed a framework that specifically identified a weekly focus for the walk-through. She suggested that as part of Jason's weekly message to his staff, he inform them of which specific belief (choice, time, relationships) he would focus his attention on for the week. The framework provided intentionality for Jason and his teachers. It also established a focus for providing authentic and formative feedback to his teachers and refined the purpose of Jason's observations.

THE BENEFITS AND PITFALLS OF FEEDBACK

Feedback is critical for student growth and learning. John Hattie (2009) in his research has posited that both timely and specific feedback have a significant impact on student learning. Hirsch (2017) posits that feedback is about providing people what they need to do the following:

- find their inner voice,
- discover their natural creativity,
- strengthen their significance, and
- stand on their own two feet. (p. 24)

Jason and Tynisha value these principles and find this to be true for providing feedback to teachers. Jason wanted the feedback to be nonevaluative, encouraging, and nonpunitive in nature. Jason also recognized the impact "in the moment" that written feedback could have on culture and morale. During several reflective conversations with Tynisha, Jason would refer to the feedback as "gumdrops and lollipops." This term was used to represent the encouraging and supportive nature of the feedback.

Therefore, he wanted the feedback to be personal. Teachers could choose to use the feedback or not; they were professionals and would make the best professional decisions. He agreed with Tynisha that a connection to the beliefs of choice, time, and relationships needed to be included in the feedback. As a result of several discussions with Tynisha, her role evolved into an accountability partner.

Tynisha, in the role of accountability partner, consistently pushed Jason to move beyond the "gumdrops and lollipops." She believed teachers needed to know what they were doing well, how the instruction aligned to the beliefs, and one area for growth. The goal of this "in-the-moment" feedback structure would also allow Jason to see where teacher strengths were as well as growth opportunities.

"GUMDROPS AND LOLLIPOPS" COME EASY

Providing teachers feedback based on "gumdrops and lollipops" is feedback anchored in positivity and glowing affirmations. It's intended to motivate, affirm, and confirm, but it must be grounded in observables, and it must be genuine. The intention is to leave teachers feeling that their hard work is paying off and they are valued as professionals. Jason loves leaving "gumdrops and lollipops." It's safe for him.

In spite of working with other administrators and Tynisha to look for elements of instructional practices grounded in balanced literacy and belief statements, Jason finds it easier to give positive feedback. It means he does not run the risk of providing instructional feedback that can be questioned by teachers who may have more expertise in literacy than he does. Tynisha and Jason spend a great deal of time discussing the "gumdrops and lollipops" approach. They agree there are benefits to this style of feedback and there are pitfalls to this style of feedback.

BENEFITS OF "GUMDROPS AND LOLLIPOPS" FEEDBACK

The main benefit of providing affirming and confirming feedback to teachers is that they feel valued for the time and energy they invest into designing rigorous and engaging lessons. Teachers also look forward to the feedback. If Jason misses a week in someone's classroom or fails to leave feedback, the teachers are left wondering. Based on feedback when he did miss an observation, Jason learned teachers were asking:

- Was everything okay?
- Did I do something wrong that you didn't want to visit?
- I was prepared for the visit. I know I'm scheduled on a Day 4.
- I miss not getting the note and the hashtag.

Teachers often stopped in his office to express how they appreciated the feedback. They were clearly communicating that they valued this feedback and that they wanted it to continue. This was especially the case if they had taken a risk with a lesson: "I was so worried about that lesson. I wasn't sure if the kids would like it. I was nervous when you walked in. But then I got your note, and it made my day," shared one teacher.

Acknowledging the hard work and professionalism helped create a climate in which teachers are willing to try new things for their students and to follow the vision and mission of the school. This bolstered the school culture around shared beliefs about literacy. Jason was becoming a literacy leader.

THE PITFALLS OF "GUMDROPS AND LOLLIPOPS" FEEDBACK

Tynisha questioned Jason when he focused too much on the affirming and confirming nature of "gumdrops and lollipops" feedback. She stressed that students need positive and yet goal-driven feedback to improve. Teachers need the same type of feedback. If teachers are never given feedback that provides a target for advanced growth, then the feedback runs the risk of being surface-level and disingenuous. It is not reality that everyone is doing a "good job" all the time. Everyone has room for improvement.

People want and need affirmation and confirmation that they are performing well. Teachers, specifically, need to know that the literacy leader has high expectations for them and is willing to support them on reaching those expectations. Jason agreed with Tynisha on all of these accounts, but he continued to struggle to know which of his teachers respond well to affirmation and which need more direct and critical feedback. Hirsch (2017) posits authentic feedback. Authentic feedback is direct and critical, but it is also about looking forward rather than focusing on the past.

GROWTH, NOT "GOTCHA"

Once literacy leaders commit to intentional observations of teaching and learning, they must help their teachers understand that this is framed in a growth mindset, not a "gotcha" mindset. Jason did this by helping his teachers understand that it was his expectation that teachers would help students grow during the year. If the expectation was for teachers to help students grow, then he committed to helping teachers grow as professionals. Observations of student learning are not "gotcha" in nature; neither are the observations of teacher learning. By affirming beliefs and stressing time, choice, and relationships, Jason communicated what he was expecting and what students deserved in terms of literacy.

CREATING A CULTURE WHERE GROWTH MOMENTS ARE WELCOME

It has been Jason's experience that teachers enjoy doing their jobs. However, recognizing growth moments can be sensitive. There can be a sense among teachers that what they do is not entirely unique compared to their peers. Some teachers rarely view themselves as a representation of how to grow and learn. Many don't see themselves as an example to their colleagues. Many teachers don't see their own success or gifts. For teachers who are excelling, they are not recognized or called on to deliver professional development or support other teachers in the building. This can be changed when the climate and culture of the building embraces student and teacher growth. Jason did this by looking for examples of student growth during his walk-throughs.

For example, if a teacher had been struggling with how to connect with a student, Jason would look for times when the student approached the teacher or had success on an assignment. He focused on the relational aspect of teaching. Then he would recognize that moment with the teacher, letting him or her know that it was through his or her effort that the student had eventually grown. Depending on the teacher and the situation, the feedback related to growth could take many forms.

For some teachers, the feedback was through a written note left after a walk-through. For others, it was a verbal acknowledgment that let them know Jason had seen their growth and appreciated their hard work. For example, if a teacher was having difficulty making read-alouds come to life, Jason would recognize varied use of intonations while he or she was reading or the technique to stop at just the right point in the book to keep the kids excited for the next day's read-aloud time.

Other times, the growth feedback was shared at a staff meeting as part of the monthly Celebrations of Superheroes among Us. Recognizing growth publicly was a risk, but Jason felt it needed to be done. The culture of the building could not change if he and his teachers were unwilling to highlight examples of growth among the ranks.

When teachers began to receive feedback that was focused on their growth, two issues emerged. The first was that teachers came to understand that Jason was interested in them as professionals. He trusted them to be autonomous and teach from a place of joy. Jason paid attention to their struggles and their successes even when it didn't look like he was paying attention. He acknowledged their hard work and sincerely appreciated it. Second, the walls of the classrooms started to crumble. Teachers began the slow and often-intimidating process of sharing their growth with each other. The sharing was informal and formal, seen and unseen, but it was present. The staff began to come together as a school, breaking through barriers of grade levels and teams.

The culture of teachers began to change. They began requesting substitutes so they could observe their colleagues teaching. Some teachers requested to observe specific teachers who they knew were having success delivering literacy lessons. Others wanted to observe another colleague's classroom management techniques. Once the first person accepted the risk of visiting a colleague's classroom, others followed.

In addition to classroom visits were discussions about literacy learning, teaching, classroom management, and planning across grade levels. These discussions were occurring at faculty meetings. During one specific meeting, a teacher recognized the knowledge he had gained from his colleagues when he spent the day observing. This teacher specifically highlighted the great pedagogy that the other teacher used. That moment seemed to unify the faculty and removed the barriers that had prevented sharing about growth previously.

The journey to be a literacy leader is fraught with many obstacles and anxious moments. Every path is different for every leader. This is just one example of a journey for one leader who is continuing to figure it out. The authors are hopeful that through this experience you will chart your own path and expand on what we have done to make a positive impact on your school and students. This chapter explores the role of feedback and how the multiplicities of the role of administrator, manager, and supervisor can be tenuous with the role of literacy leader.

Chapter 9, the final chapter of this text, connects all the chapters under three main beliefs: time, relationships, and choice. The authors have found these three values to be crucial to the ongoing development of the elementary literacy leader. These values are connected to the key themes explored throughout the text. In this final chapter, the authors present an honest case on the challenges as well as the successes of being a literacy leader who leads from these three beliefs.

REFLECTION QUESTIONS

- Think of a time when you realized you didn't know what you needed to know. How was feedback provided to you?
- What sources provided that feedback to you?
- Reflect on the feedback you provide to teachers. How has your feedback been focused, intentional, and timely?
- How can you find time in your day to visit classrooms?
- Who can you identify as your accountability partner to ensure you prioritize classroom walk-throughs?
- What is one way you can ensure you create a culture where walk-throughs are not perceived as punitive?

REFERENCES

Bickmore, D. L., & Sulentic Dowell, M-M. (2011). Concerns, use of time, and the intersections of leadership: Case study of two charter school principals. *Research in the Schools, 18*(1), 44–61.

Booth, D., & Rowsell, J. (2007). *The literacy principal, leading, supporting, and assessing reading and writing initiatives* (2nd ed.). Portland, ME: Stenhouse.

Hallinger, P. (2003). Leading educational change: Reflections on the practice of instructional and transformational leadership. *Cambridge Journal of Education, 33*(3), 329–351. doi: 10.1080/0305764032000122005

Hallinger, P. (2011). A review of three decades of doctoral studies using the principal instructional management rating scale: A lens on methodological progress in educational leadership. *Educational Administration Quarterly, 47*(2), 271–306.

Hallinger, P., & Heck, R. H. (2002). What do we call people with vision? The role of vision, mission and goals in school leadership and improvement. In K. A. Leithwood (Ed.), *Second international handbook of educational leadership and administration* (pp. 9–40). Dordrecht; Boston, MA: Kluwer.

Hallinger, P., & Murphy, J. (1985). Assessing the instructional management behavior of principals. *Elementary School Journal, 86*(2), 217–247.

Hattie, J. (2009). *Visible learning: A synthesis of over 800 meta-analyses relating to achievement.* New York, NY: Routledge.

Hirsch, J. (2017). *The feedback fix: Dump the past, embrace the future, and lead the way to change.* Lanham, MD: Rowman & Littlefield.

Hoewing, B., & Sulentic Dowell, M-M. (2010). The elementary principal as chief literacy officer: Myth, legend, fairy tale or reality? *Journal of the Southern Regional Council of Educational Administration,* 63–73.

Leithwood, K. A., Louis, K. S., Anderson, S., & Wahlstrom, K. (2004). *How leadership influences student learning: Review of research.* Toronto, Canada: Center of Applied Research and Educational Improvement; Ontario Institute for Studies in Education, University of Toronto.

Sulentic Dowell, M-M. (2012). Addressing the complexities of literacy and urban teaching in the United States: Strategic professional development as intervention. *Teaching Education Journal, 23*(1), 40–49.

Sulentic Dowell, M-M., Hoewing, B., & Bickmore, D. (2012). A framework for defining literacy leadership. *Journal of Reading Education, 37*(2), 7–15.

Weston, D. (2014). *Teacher workload diary survey.* Teacher Development Trust. Retrieved from https://tdtrust.org/10-things-you-need-to-know-about-the-teacher-workload-survey-

Zepeda, S. J. (2007). *The principal as instructional leader: A handbook for supervisors.* Larchmont, NY: Eye on Education.

Chapter Nine

Where Do We Go from Here?

The role of the elementary principal has changed. In fact, it will continue to evolve as education continues to meet the demands of students, as the teaching profession advances, and as shifts in U.S. society impact and influence teaching and learning. Research will also affect the role of instructional leaders in elementary settings.

Specific to literacy leadership, Sulentic Dowell, Bickmore, and Hoewing (2012) first described the evolution of the principal within the context of instructional leadership versus administrative or strictly managerial leadership. Upon this work, a framework for literacy leadership at the elementary level was established. Presented in chapter 2 of this text, this literacy leadership framework addresses the literacy knowledge elementary principals need in order to be literacy leaders who support teacher autonomy and instill joy into teaching spaces.

As an elementary principal, Jason saw this need for himself, for he did not enter his role as elementary principal with the literacy knowledge to be an effective literacy leader. Recognizing that he was lacking necessary literacy content knowledge and pedagogical expertise, Jason addressed his dearth of understanding directly. One example is when he enrolled in a guided reading-assessment course *with* his teachers. The course was taught by Tara, the literacy coach, and Amy, the director of curriculum for the school district. Doing so exposed his vulnerability, but also demonstrated his commitment to becoming a literacy leader.

Taking the course was an intimidating experience for Jason. He was the lone administrator in the course with thirty to thirty-five elementary teachers from both of the district's elementary schools. Tara and Amy knew Jason was apprehensive. When it came time to have the teachers work in small groups, they made sure to place him in a group with teachers who would be supportive of his lack of knowledge.

Reading the material and discussing his learning with his small group posed little concern. Sharing with the whole group and explaining the concepts of guided reading was a great source of trepidation. It was anxiety-provoking because in that moment he had to share his lack of knowledge. He was the principal, the leader, the champion of literacy, and he knew very little about it. He worried that the teachers would view him as incompetent and lose faith in his vision. While sharing his learning in front of the entire group was terrifying, so was having to give informal running records to students and create guided reading lessons for the students.

Jason was given a student to work with during the course. Tara and Amy knew he was nervous, so they provided tutoring to Jason. They allowed him to watch them give informal running records. He then gave running records with them observing. They scored the running records together and determined the needs of the student. Although the course has ended, Jason continues to meet with the student weekly to read and play games.

While Jason would not consider himself an expert on guided reading, he does believe he understands it better and can give feedback about guided reading lessons when he does his classroom walk-throughs. He also knows that the teachers accept his feedback because they know he took the guided reading class. Most of all, he did the learning alongside his teachers.

The elementary principal assumes many roles and responsibilities that span the spectrum of supervision, leadership, and management. Literacy leadership extends beyond being the traditional instructional leader. As authors, we recognize there are many instructional leaders in the building. A literacy leader understands the multifaceted aspects of literacy learning at the elementary level and recognizes that literacy lives in all areas of instruction and classroom culture.

Traditional principal and school leadership programs are not constructed in ways that promote the development of an elementary school principal to assume the responsibility of being a literacy leader. In some schools and districts, elementary principals have thrown up their hands and given all things literacy to the literacy coach, reading specialist(s), interventionist, or district-level curriculum development officer. As Jason would say, and Tynisha and Margaret-Mary would agree, this is a travesty.

Routman (2014) highlights that the majority of school leaders in charge of literacy often do not have a background in literacy instruction or literacy leadership. This can create an abyss of skills when the school leader is charged with building and sustaining a culture that supports literacy instruction in the school and has little or no specific training related to literacy. While the dearth of knowledge related to literacy leadership can be seen as a weakness, a school leader who works collaboratively with teachers to develop a shared belief system and develop a literacy mission and vision has the capacity to transform the culture.

Elementary principals may claim they are asked to do things they are largely unequipped to do or don't have time to do, such as visiting teachers' classrooms on a daily basis and giving feedback, as described in chapter 8. The authors of this text argue that if elementary principals do not assume the role of literacy leaders, then the risks and consequences of failure are high for everyone, but especially high for children.

EMBRACING A CULTURE OF JOY

The authors focused on culture and climate in chapter 2. They took a deep dive into joy in chapter 3. Tynisha, Jason, and Margaret-Mary posit that joy, as a cornerstone of culture, will change how teachers see themselves as professionals, will create an environment where students want to come to school and learn, and will create a place and space where parents know that learning is taking place every day. Joy is not temporary; it is what visitors feel when they walk through the door.

Joy occurs when the literacy leader creates a culture where everyone is free to be their authentic self. This level of authenticity invites teachers to engage in literacy practices that encourage both teachers and students to think differently. Teachers are encouraged to think outside of the box and create learning opportunities that engage students, to build their literacy skills, and to view literacy as a means to acquire knowledge. This involves risk-taking.

In order for teachers to think outside of the box, the culture must be open to risk-taking and creative thinking, so that there isn't consequence for thinking differently, wanting to try new pedagogies, or not wanting to use the prescribed curriculum. Options are necessary for teachers and students to feel a sense of joy. In Jason's schools, this is called choice.

KEEP IT SIMPLE—JUST TEACH

Maybe this is easier said than done, but the role of teacher has become complicated. The reality is that individuals don't aspire to become teachers anymore. Negative press and negative perceptions work against the profession and have influenced how individuals perceive the role of the teacher. Many would rather pursue another career option that is perceived as prestigious. The charge for the literacy leader is to create the conditions for the early career teachers to stay in the profession and for the veteran teachers to be reminded daily why they have committed their lives to this work.

In order to let teachers teach, we must give them autonomy. The ability of individuals to have autonomy in their jobs has revealed a positive impact on their creativity, production, and job satisfaction (Pink, 2009). Teachers who report higher levels of autonomy within the classroom often also report higher levels of job satisfaction. However, recent evidence may suggest that teachers are losing the ability to make decisions related to instructional materials, educational policy, and pedagogical choices within the classroom. The amount of autonomy teachers experience is declining. Some even suggest that the loss of autonomy is what is driving teachers from the profession (Boser & Hanna, 2014).

Of all public school teachers, teachers at the elementary level report having the lowest level of autonomy. The responsibility of increased or decreased autonomy falls in the hands of the literacy leader. This individual has the ability to create the culture and assume the responsibility where teaching occurs. Ingersoll notes in an interview with Tim Walker (2016), "Teachers are micromanaged. They have been saying for a long time that one size *doesn't* fit all. All students are different. But they are told to stick to the scripted curriculum which might work for a weaker teacher but it drives good teachers nuts." Unfortunately, this powerful statement has garnered attention from other authors who do not share the same viewpoint on teacher autonomy.

IT MAY NOT WORK

As school leaders, literacy leaders, teachers, and scholars, we know the reality is that this may not work for every building, every district, and every school leader. As authors, we are aware of the challenges and the implications that the political landscape has on schools. However, this is not an excuse not to try. Jason would say that trying is easy; maintaining is hard. He is fortunate to work in a district that has exceptional school board support and district-level support. It is not uncommon for teachers to be invited to present at school board meetings and be asked if they have all the resources they need to improve literacy.

If the school board receives the impression that teachers need more materials or professional development, they allocate the financial resources to get the materials in teachers' and students' hands. The superintendent, business manager, and director of curriculum in Jason's district are equally supportive. They always make sure that the teachers and students have what they need to be successful. Cost is a secondary concern, not the primary motivation.

Despite having school-board and district-level leadership support, Jason finds it difficult to maintain the initiatives related to teacher joy and autonomy: "So many things get in the way, and it's not any one person. It's just everything." Jason hears this a great deal from his teachers. He feels it and lives it, too. When he hears a teacher say this or when he says this to himself, he would love to think, *Well, it's just been a long day, and he and the teacher need a little pep talk.*

It will take more than a pep talk to fix the loss of autonomy and subsequent loss of joy. Teachers do experience joy throughout their day. During the great moments when they make instructional decisions in the best interests of their students, there is an immense feeling of joy. Jason is lucky enough to observe this often, but not often enough. When teachers make the choice to deviate from the scripted curriculum and make a personal connection with their students, there is observable joy. Jason witnesses this all the time in the classrooms in his building as his teachers exercise their choice, rely on their expertise and professional judgment, and rely on their professional decision-making.

The feeling of joy is more often than not short lived, like a fleeting moment. At the beginning of the school year, there is great excitement and joy. But as the demands of benchmark assessments, data digs, and accountability measures begin to amass, the joy begins to fade away.

Jason compares this to storm clouds that cover the sun on a glorious Wisconsin summer day. He thinks of these moments as the gathering storm clouds of guilt that come rolling in to obliterate that sunshine. Teachers express to Jason their worry that because they veered from the scripted scope, sequence, and pace of the curriculum, they have now somehow set their students' learning behind. They doubt their own professional judgment, knowledge, and expertise, second-guessing themselves and thinking that as they are not "on pace" anymore, that cannot be good. When this happens—when autonomy is lost—joy evaporates.

The teachers are not the only ones in the building who feel the storm clouds of guilt. Jason also experiences this. Sometimes, it follows him home at night, the feeling invades his thoughts, and he is haunted. As much as he believes in the professional decision-making of his teachers, and he recognizes and acknowledges the need for his teachers to have instructional autonomy, and knows his students and teachers need to experience joyful learning, there is fear.

Jason reveals that sometimes, he fears that he is leading his staff down the wrong path. What if his vision is wrong? What if they are going down the wrong track? His thinking can get wild as he wonders, "What if I—if we—screw up the kids and their learning suffers?" What if a skills-based, one-size-fits-all, prepackaged, scripted curriculum is the best way to reach kids?

When Jason begins thinking about these questions, it is challenging to maintain the path of a true literacy leader. He also believes that there is comfort in doing what we have always done. While students may not have excelled, we knew they were learning. They could read, write, and complete math problems to some degree of proficiency; the tests told us that, right? They may not have found joy or choice in their learning, but at least the test scores were satisfactory.

Jason knows his teachers feel this, too. There is comfort in a curriculum that is scripted. They then don't have to worry about making a mistake with their students. Recalling the words of Jason's teacher, Maria, from earlier in the book, "I want autonomy and choice, but it is just easier if you tell us what to do." Maria is not a lazy teacher. She is passionate and engaging and puts in countless hours of effort—often at the expense of her own family—to make sure her students get her best every day. At times she's struggling to keep up.

Every year there is a new initiative, even when Jason says there will be no change. Maria ascribes to the reading beliefs of choice, time, and relationships, but how can she do it with so many other demands? At the beginning of the year, when she's supposed to be establishing community and relationships, she has to pull her students to complete her benchmark assessments so she has data for fall collaboration. She laments, "If I'm supposed to be building relationships through books, do we really mean we are going to do that through assessments? It just doesn't make sense." No, it does not.

What else gets in the way are the constant changes in policy and mandates passed down from the federal and state governments. Jason and his teachers can't keep up. They really do know what their students need. They live in the community with the parents, work with students at school, and send their own children to their elementary school. Together, Jason and the teachers with whom he works are committed to providing excellent learning opportunities for all students. They developed the literacy beliefs of choice, time, and relationships. They have been focused, passionate, and ready to move forward. And then, a new mandate comes along, and they are faced with another hurdle that undermines their beliefs.

Jason and his teachers want to push back; they are tired: tired of fighting, tired of getting their hopes up that they can have autonomy and joy only to be told by the policy-makers, politicians, test-prep industry, and commercial curriculum companies that they have to do it their way. Yet Jason and his teachers keep holding on to the reading beliefs and their commitment to autonomy and joy. They know their school, their kids, and their community. What keeps Jason focused is something his school district's attorney once told him: "I can always defend your actions if you have acted in the best interest of your students." So that keeps him going. While this is not easy, Jason didn't sign up for easy. He signed up to be the literacy leader of his campus.

Good and bad moments happen in the life of a literacy leader. The authors believe the following are reasons why bad moments may be superseding good moments. They are listed so that readers of this text can compare these ideas to their own experiences. Here are the ways the authors have experienced a loss of autonomy, trust, and joy and how their relationships have been impacted by a forfeiture of choice and inadequate time for teaching and learning.

- Policy gets in the way;
- Balancing district mandates with what is best for your building; and
- The balance of specific building needs such as:

   1. teacher needs,
   2. staff needs,
   3. student needs,
   4. family needs, and
   5. community needs.

FINAL THOUGHTS

The recurring themes in this text related to literacy leadership were joy, autonomy, and trust and in regard to teaching, relationships, choice, and time. Teacher autonomy is at the core of this text. Boser and Hanna (2014) add credence and support Carey's (2008) view that teachers do enjoy a high level of autonomy. Their data suggest that teachers are experiencing some of the highest levels of autonomy and job satisfaction of any time in recent history. Boser and Hanna (2014) argue that it is the freedom of choice that teachers have that hurts the profession and prevents teachers from perfecting what they teach.

If policy-makers didn't try to control education for profit, but rather, teachers and principals, coaches, and curriculum directors, in tandem with families and communities, better defined what should be taught and what students should learn, there would be radical improvement in the public school systems in the United States. As career educators, we argue that less autonomy, not more, is needed. However, less autonomy does not equate to less support. Boser and Hanna (2014) strongly support a model that is grounded in more professional development to perfect their teaching. They argue for increased time for collaborative professional development opportunities.

The practice of quality professional development for teachers has been employed by many of the high-performing nations. Teachers in these contexts report high levels of job satisfaction despite working in some of the most poverty-stricken areas in what may seem like adverse working conditions that are seemingly beyond challenging. To combat this, Boser and

Hanna (2014) argue that policy-makers should make a concerted effort to increase pay and improve conditions for teachers.

In addition to autonomy, there is joy. The feeling of joy is a result of the school culture, a shared sense of self-worth and satisfaction with making work decisions. The school culture is created by the principal, particularly one who assumes the role of literacy leader who works in collaboration with teachers and his or her community. School culture is driven by a core set of beliefs that drive decision-making, in addition to test data. While autonomy has been shown to have a strong impact on job satisfaction and productivity, shared beliefs of a school staff is a needed partner of autonomy.

British scholar Sammons (1995) reviewed school effectiveness research and identified eleven specific factors of effective schools. The second factor for an effective school is a *shared vision and goals*. Within that factor is included unity of purpose, consistency of practice, and collegiality and collaboration.

Having a set of core beliefs related to reading and literacy is supported by Routman (2014). Routman highlights the need for a school to have a shared set of beliefs for literacy. Those core literacy beliefs are used to drive the instructional decisions made when determining curriculum and materials. Routman (2014) states, "What teachers believe about a concept, an instructional approach, or a learning process greatly influences their degree of openness to new concepts, their flexibility, and their willingness to commit to new ideas" (p. 83).

Without a set of shared core literacy beliefs, teachers lose focus, and what may look like autonomy may, in fact, be confusion, causing teachers to make their own decisions without a belief framework to guide them. Without a framework, a classroom teacher's ability to experience autonomy in instructional decision-making as well as creating a joyful learning environment may be significantly compromised.

The authors recognize that both autonomy and joy are favorable teaching conditions, and they understand how autonomy and joy interface. They acknowledge that time, choice, and relationships are pivotal components to teaching and learning. The literature from the fields of teaching, teacher education, and educational leadership points to the influence of each as well as to how a literacy leader provides the instruction leadership necessary for success.

Wolk (2008) notes that to create joy in learning, students should be given choice in what they experience in the classroom. And McAndrew (2005) identifies the importance of creating a school culture that is fundamentally supportive of teachers. A significant aspect of supporting teachers is welcoming and encouraging their voices (Birnam & Nary, 2013). As choice motivates students toward higher levels of engagement, the authors posit that choice also empowers teachers and serves as a rich source of inspiration. In a culture where support is readily accessible and acts as a stimulus, a commonly held belief system around literacy instructional practice encourages teachers to take calculated risks when making instructional decisions. In this culture framework, the school leader must have fundamental trust that the teachers are competent in their abilities (Gostick & Elton, 2012).

The authors of this book have all experienced the joy that comes from being supported and enabled to make informed classroom, building-level, and district-wide decisions. They have experienced autonomy and a paucity of autonomy. As career educators, they know the value of choice, time, and relationships in teaching and learning. Tynisha, Jason, and Margaret-Mary have felt and recognized joy.

As authors, they hope that reading this text causes readers, especially literacy leaders, to reflect on their leadership and practices and to rediscover their reasons for entering the teaching profession. Education is a promise for many of our students to attain literacy equity. A quality teacher is needed in every elementary classroom. In addition, a strong literacy leader is needed to support the success of every teacher, family, and student.

REFLECTION QUESTIONS

- How have you experimented with new ideas and taken risks in your building as a literacy leader?
- How can you create a culture where risk-taking is celebrated?
- Where do you see trust and collaboration?
- What are two or three actions you can employ to build trust and collaboration among teachers and other school leadership?
- What are your next steps as a literacy leader to transform yourself through reflection and learning?

REFERENCES

Birnam, E., & Nary, D. (2013). *When teacher voices are heard: The future of the literacy landscape.* Lanham, MD: Rowman & Littlefield Education.

Boser, U., & Hanna, R. (2014). In the quest to improve schools, have teachers been stripped of their autonomy? *Center for American Progress.*

Carey, K. (2008). The teacher autonomy paradox. *The American Prospect.*

Gostick, A., & Elton, C. (2012). *All in: How the best managers create a culture of belief and drive big results.* New York, NY: Simon and Schuster.

McAndrew, D. A. (2005) *Literacy leadership: Six strategies for peoplework.* Newark, DE: International Reading Association.

Pink, D. (2009). *Drive: The surprising truth about what motivates us.* New York, NY: Riverhead.

Routman, R. (2014). *Read, write, lead: Breakthrough strategies for schoolwide literacy success.* Alexandria, VA: ASCD.

Sammons, P. (1995). *Key characteristics of effective schools: A review of school effectiveness research.* London, England: B & MBC Distribution Services.

Sulentic Dowell, M-M., Bickmore, D., & Hoewing, B. (2012). A framework for defining literacy leadership. *Journal of Reading Education, 37*(2), 7–15.

Walker, T. (2016). *Teacher autonomy declined over past decade, new data shows.* Blog post. Retrieved from http://neatoday.org/2016/01/11/teacher-autonomy-in-the-classroom

Wolk, S. (2008, September). Joy in school. *Educational Leadership, 66*(1), 8–15.

About the Authors

Tynisha D. Meidl, Ph.D., is associate professor of teacher education at St. Norbert College in De Pere, Wisconsin, where she also serves as the co-chair of the teacher education program. Meidl's research agenda is informed by her experiences as a teacher in urban and rural contexts. Her research is specific to literacy development within the context of teacher development, inclusive classroom culture, culturally relevant curriculum, service-learning, and literacy leadership. Meidl teaches literacy courses focused on assisting pre-service teachers to enter the classroom as proficient literacy teachers. Prior to joining the faculty at St. Norbert, she taught in the Baltimore City Public Schools and in the Rio Grande Valley in Texas. Meidl is a Teach for America alumna and current co-editor of the *Literacy and Social Responsibility ejournal*. She is the co-founder of District Literacy Leadership (DiLL) SIG of the International Literacy Association (ILA), as well as the co-founder of VIDA charter school in Pennsylvania. She has authored multiple book chapters and journal articles on issues ranging from instructional approaches to culturally diverse classrooms to service learning in urban contexts. Meidl earned her Ph.D. in curriculum and instruction from Pennsylvania State University.

Jason Lau, Ph.D., is the principal at Westwood Elementary School and at the Phantom Knight School of Opportunity (a project-based charter school) for the school district of West De Pere in De Pere, Wisconsin. Lau assumes many responsibilities in his role as a dual principal, including facilitating mission and vision and providing teacher autonomy. Prior to becoming a principal, he was a school psychologist for the Milwaukee Public School District and the Kohler School District. He has served in the capacity of director of students services for the school district of Kohler and the school

117

district of West De Pere. Lau has presented at national and regional conferences on various issues related to literacy leadership. He lends his expertise to the District Literacy Leadership (DiLL) SIG of the International Literacy Association (ILA) as webmaster and rural literacy contact. Lau earned a master's degree in school psychology from the University of Wisconsin–Whitewater and his Ph.D. in leadership and policy analysis from the University of Wisconsin–Madison.

Margaret-Mary Sulentic Dowell, Ph.D., is Cecil "Pete" Taylor Endowed Professor of Literacy and Urban Education at Louisiana State University, Baton Rouge, where she also serves as director of the LSU Writing Project and coordinator of the elementary grades 1–5 Teacher Education Program. Sulentic Dowell's research agenda is focused broadly on literacy in urban and rural settings, specifically the complexities of literacy leadership; providing access to literature, writing, and the arts; and service learning as a pathway to preparing pre-service teachers to teach literacy authentically in urban environs. Sulentic Dowell spent fifteen years as an educator in the Waterloo, Iowa, community schools and taught in rural districts in Iowa and Minnesota. Sulentic Dowell was a service-learning faculty fellow at the University of Southern Mississippi, Hattiesburg, and co-founder of District Literacy Leadership (DiLL) SIG of the International Literacy Association (ILA). She is also former assistant superintendent for sixty-four elementary schools in the East Baton Rouge Parish School System. Sulentic Dowell earned her Ph.D. in curriculum and instruction, specializing in literacy studies at the University of Iowa.

Made in the USA
Coppell, TX
08 April 2022

76251093R00083